Praise for

Simply Delicious Amish Cooking

Sherry Gore's simple, mouth-watering recipes, plus enjoyable stories about the Plain community in Sarasota, Florida, make this cookbook interesting, unique, and a definite keeper.

Wanda E. Brunstetter, *New York Times* bestselling author
of *The Half-Stitched Amish Quilting Club*

Sherry Gore's *Simply Delicious Amish Cooking* is a heartwarming glimpse into the Pinecraft Community, complete with tender stories and scrumptious recipes. It will delight fans of Amish fiction and readers who love the Plain culture.

Amy Clipston, bestselling author of
the *Kauffman Amish Bakery Series*

Simply Delicious Amish Cooking by Sherry Gore is a collection of wonderful, straightforward, and easy-to-follow recipes, but it's the stories and tips that make this cookbook a treasure trove. Along with expanding your repertoire of recipes, you'll discover a new side to Florida: Pinecraft, a tiny village made up of fascinating Plain people ... who love to cook.

Suzanne Woods Fisher, bestselling author of books
about the Old Order Amish, including
Amish Peace: *Simple Wisdom for a Complicated World*

Simply Delicious Amish Cooking is more than just a book of hearty, home-style recipes. It gives the reader a seat at the supper table in a home dedicated to God and good food, hands over a number of good dishes interspersed with vignettes and stories about a community where lives are filled with peace that passes understanding, and bids farewell with a warm hug.

Nancy E. Turner, author of *These Is My Words*

What do you give to a friend who has everything? A cookbook by Sherry Gore, of course! Sherry's cookbook, *Simply Delicious Amish Cooking*, is a unique blend of homespun stories and delicious recipes that would appeal to most anyone. I enjoy thumbing through the pages, reading *The Budget* entries, and feeling like I too am getting a taste of Pinecraft.

Shelley Shepard Gray, *New York Times*
and *USA Today* bestselling author

Simply Delicious Amish Cooking is a treasure filled with scrumptious recipes, gorgeous photos, and delightful stories! This cookbook is a treat, and every person who enjoys getting a peek into the Plain life will be glad they own it! I plan to purchase copies for my daughters-in-law and for grandchildren who are not yet born. It's *that* good.

Cindy Woodsmall, *New York Times* bestselling
author of *When the Soul Mends*

Simply Delicious Amish Cooking by Sherry Gore is *simply amazing*! This will quickly become my go-to cookbook. (Chocolate Whoopie Pies, yum!) But my favorite part is Sherry's stories sprinkled throughout the book. Sherry brings the Amish community of Pinecraft to life within these pages, bumping it up to the TOP of my vacation wishlist. This is a cookbook you'll want to indulge in ... just like the recipes within its pages.

Tricia Goyer, bestselling author of
34 books, including the Seven Brides
for Seven Bachelors Amish Series

Simply Delicious
AMISH COOKING

Recipes and Stories from the Amish of Sarasota, Florida

by SHERRY GORE

ZONDERVAN®

ZONDERVAN.com/
AUTHORTRACKER
follow your favorite authors

ZONDERVAN

Simply Delicious Amish Cooking
Copyright © 2013 by Sherry Gore

Portions of this book were previously published in *Taste of Pinecraft*.

This title is also available as a Zondervan ebook. Visit www.zondervan.com/ebooks.

Requests for information should be addressed to:
Zondervan, *Grand Rapids, Michigan 49530*

ISBN 978-0-310-33554-2

Published in association with the Steve Laube Agency.

Cover design: Michelle Lenger
Cover photography: Chris Meyer / Memories by Chris
Interior photography: Chris Meyer / Memories by Chris
Interior design: Beth Shagene
Editorial: Carolyn McCready and Bob Hudson

Printed in the United States of America

13 14 15 16 17 18 19 20 /CHM/ 22 21 20 19 18 17 16 15 14 13 12 11 10 9 8 7 6 5 4 3 2 1

To my bishop, Lester Gingerich,
my church family at Sunnyside Amish Mennonite Church,
and the remarkable folks of Pinecraft.
Home is where they love you.

Special thanks to Cindy and Suzanne for believing in me,
and to Tab, my biggest supporter.

Contents

Introduction

Introduction

How I Came to Write This Cookbook

Life was chaotic. My daughter Jacinda was sick in the hospital in St. Petersburg, Florida, an hour's drive away, and my young son, Tyler, needed me at home. Daughter Shannon was fifteen at the time — too young to drive but bearing great responsibility by working at Yoder's Restaurant to help support the family. My days were spent keeping other people's houses clean and attempting to be in too many places at one time.

I prayed for help.

I shouldn't have been surprised when a friend called me the next day. She had a cousin in Chihuahua, Mexico, she said, who was looking for a family to assist in the United States. Would I like her cousin to come and help me?

Within the week, two planes passed in the night — one from El Paso, Texas, and the other, a Mercy Medical flight destined for Cincinnati, Ohio, where Jacinda would receive treatment at the children's hospital.

Rosy Banman, our helper from Mexico, was the daughter of a Russian Mennonite minister. Though she was young, only nineteen, she was amazingly efficient. Not only did she keep everything running smoothly in my absence, but her quiet spirit delighted those who came in contact with her.

A week before returning to Mexico, Rosy presented me with a gift — a cookbook from her Mennonite community. I had planned to send Rosy home with the usual souvenirs, Florida oranges or key-lime-and-coconut candies, bought locally, but I also wanted to send her off with an Amish cookbook from our own community. I scoured Pinecraft for such a book, going from store to store, but I came away empty-handed. No such item was available because none had ever been written.

So after Rosy left, I began compiling my own cookbook. My good friend Vera Overholt helped in the effort by handing out recipe cards to Pinecraft women on which to write their recipes. After I mentioned the project in my letters to *The Budget* newspaper, many ladies in Amish communities across the country responded. All of the recipes in this book are by residents of Pinecraft or those who have vacationed here. Pinecraft is a popular vacation spot for many Amish and Mennonites.

Little did I know it would take three years to finish my cookbook. Much of it was written in a hospital room, and several times I had to put my work away and concentrate on caring for Jacinda, whose health continues to be fragile. Nearly seven hundred recipes and three years' worth of excerpts from "Letters from Home" in the national edition of *The Budget* newspaper went into that first cookbook, *Taste of Pinecraft*. The book you hold in your hands, containing more than three hundred recipes, is culled from that original collection, with many new recipes included.

The excerpts interspersed among the recipes in this book give only a glimpse of life in Pinecraft. No book could capture every element and every character that comprises our unique settlement.

What Makes Amish Cooking So Special?

Amish cooking is traditional American cooking at its best, and like America itself, Amish cooking includes a lot of international flavors. Some recipes even have German and Dutch names, and some Mexican-American and even Italian recipes will be found in these pages.

Amish cooking is defined by simplicity. With only a few exceptions — like alligator meat! — these recipes require only the most basic commonly available ingredients, what some people refer to as "whole" foods. In the ingredients lists you will not find things like "chipotle chilies in adobo sauce" or "cold-pressed extra virgin olive oil," as good as those things may be. These recipes, like the Amish themselves, are straightforward and plain, but never boring. That is why this book is called *Simply Delicious Amish Cooking*.

From the various clippings from *The Budget* scattered throughout this book, you'll also notice that food is a special part of Amish social life. It is served at potlucks, marriage services, special events, fundraisers, and farewells. Wherever the community gathers, food will be abundant.

Food is also one of the ways we reach out to the larger world. We make visitors, whether old friends or strangers, feel welcome. Sharing food is how we support one another in difficult times and show our love to those in need. It is a gesture of our caring for each other and, ultimately, an expression of how God loves us and provides for our needs. Amish food is not just food, it's a reminder of our dependence on a loving God.

Who Are the Amish and Mennonites?

The people known as the Amish first organized between 1693 and 1697 when a Mennonite leader named Jacob Ammann and a minority group of followers in Switzerland divided from the main body of Mennonites. Ammann held a strict view of excommunication and the banning of offending believers from the church.

A small group of Dutch Mennonites had previously settled in Germantown, Pennsylvania, in 1683, and greater numbers began arriving in the United States in 1710. The earliest Amish immigrants to the New World arrived in Pennsylvania about 1720, settling in Berks County and later in Lancaster County.

The Amish largely agree with the Mennonites in doctrine but even today still hold to a strict observance of excommunication and a stricter pattern of dress than the Mennonites. They "withhold" from making lifestyle changes, choosing to drive horses and buggies rather than cars and usually shunning modern conveniences. Today, the largest concentration of Amish is in Holmes County, Ohio.

Today the true Mennonite Church (Mennonite and Amish Mennonite) is still a separatist church and is neither Catholic nor Protestant. They believe in the following Bible principles:

1. A full obedience and discipleship to Christ and all his commandments, resulting in holy living (Matthew 7:21; Acts 5:32; 1 John 2:4 – 6)

2. Love for enemies, nonresistance to evil, nonparticipation in war (Matthew 5:38 – 39; James 5:5 – 6; 1 Peter 3:13 – 18)

3. A true separation of church and state as "strangers and pilgrims" (1 Peter 2:11 – 12)

4. Baptism for believers only (Mark 16:31)

5. Inspiration of the Bible in its entirety (2 Timothy 3:16)

6. Nonswearing of oaths (Matthew 5:33 – 37; James 5:12)

7. Modesty and simplicity of attire, and nonadornment with jewelry, etc. (1 Peter 3:3 – 4; 1 Timothy 2:9)

8. Recognition of God's order of headship and the wearing of veiling for sisters (1 Corinthians 11:1 – 6)

9. Marriage as instituted of God, sacred, and for life (Matthew 19:3 – 6; Hebrews 13:4)

10. The sanctity of sex. That young people keep themselves pure (Ephesians 5:3 – 5) and that they marry only Christian partners (2 Corinthians 6:14 – 18)

11. The "kiss of charity" practiced among believers (Romans 16:16; 1 Peter 5:14)

12. The anointing of oil for the sick (James 5:14 – 15)

13. Feet washing among the believers (John 13)

14. Lawsuits, secret societies, labor unions, and life insurance as unscriptural (Psalm 37:25; Jeremiah 49:11; Matthew 6:25 – 33; 1 Corinthians 6:1 – 8; 2 Corinthians 6:14 – 18; Ephesians 5:11 – 12)

15. Security of the believer conditional — if we continue in the faith unto the end (Hebrews 3:6, 14)

What Is the Pinecraft Community?

Unknown to many around the country today, there is a thriving Amish and Mennonite community in Sarasota, Florida. In 1926 the original Pinecraft community was laid out on the southwest corner of Bahia Vista and South Kaufman Streets. It was originally designed for a trailer park with lots that were 40 feet by 40 feet along with some small cottages. In 1928, when the Dan Kurtz and Roman Miller families moved to this area, they began to hold Amish German Sunday school in their homes, and preaching services were held when a minister came by. Later, as more Amish and Mennonite families came for the winter, a schoolhouse was used for services but was soon outgrown.

In about 1937 services were conducted in English because some Mennonites could not speak German, though a German Sunday school class was still available for those who preferred German. When a minister was present, he was asked to preach after Sunday school whether he was Amish, Conservative Mennonite, or Mennonite.

In 1945, after the continued growth of the community, a group of Mennonites wanted to live in the area permanently, so they organized the Bay Shore Mennonite Church under the Ohio Conference.

In the meantime, Henry Brunk bought a tourist camp on U.S. 41 at the north end of Sarasota. There was a good-sized community building on it where tourists assembled for worship services. In 1946, as the need for more space became evident, a vacant bakery was purchased, renovated, and named the Tourist Church as a joint fellowship of Amish, Conservative Mennonites, and Mennonites. Services were held only during the winter. Since more folks wanted to stay year round, they organized under the Lancaster Conference, using the same building. Down through the years, many folks expressed their appreciation for the Tourist Church, where folks from the North and from many different faiths fellowshipped together, saying this was a foretaste of heaven.

Some of the early Pinecraft and Home Croft settlers bought lots and built small, plain buildings where they were kept warm and dry. Others put up nice-looking cottages. Gradually as the years rolled by, better homes were built. Eventually many of the early shacks had to be torn down or remodeled.

Ed Yoder started a grocery store and also sold meat on the corner of

Bahia Vista and Kaufman Streets, which was a great asset to the area. Mart Yoder and John Yutzy opened a hardware store, which was also greatly needed. Soon a post office was added to Yoder Grocery store, and a restaurant called the Eating House came into being.

The Sunnyside Church was started about 1969 or 1970, being organized under the nonconference Amish Mennonite Fellowship and later merged with the Beachy Amish Fellowship with Lester Gingerich as resident bishop and John F. Miller and Harvey Miller ordained as deacons.

Today in Pinecraft, fishing, playing shuffleboard and marble games, quilting, and making shell crafts keeps many residents occupied. Also, many women are engaged in doing house cleaning in the city.

What Is *The Budget*?

Over the years, *The Budget* newspaper has earned a faithful readership by providing its Amish and Mennonite readers with a place where the good news reported in its pages routinely outweighs the bad. It is the most popular and widely read local weekly newspaper in the heart of Ohio's Amish country, and its readers have helped to shape this book. Most of the vignettes and stories scattered throughout this book were first published in *The Budget*.

Established in 1890, *The Budget* is a community paper in the purest sense, giving its readers content that mirrors their lifestyles and successfully brings together the workplace, marketplace, and church, the English and the Plain People. Its local pages are filled with timely and insightful news stories, compelling human-interest features, inspirational messages from area pastors and their congregations, deserving acknowledgments of academic achievements and extracurricular activities, and the most comprehensive local school sports coverage.

The Budget, however, is also known nationally and internationally. Its national edition publishes letters by Amish and Mennonite writers, representing their communities throughout the United States (primarily Ohio, Indiana, and Pennsylvania), as well as Canada, Central and South America, and overseas.

Out of respect for its 116-year relationship with our Amish and Mennonite writers, readers, and friends, the national edition remains available only in its print format, although you can find highlights of each weekly local edition online at thebudgetnewspaper.com. For information or to subscribe, write *The Budget*, PO Box 249, Sugarcreek, OH 44681. You may also phone 330-852-4634 or fax 330-852-4421. (The information given above about *The Budget* was largely adapted from *The Budget*'s website with the permission of its publisher.)

The Recipes

Breads and Rolls

Honey Wheat Bread

¼ cup flour

¼ cup sugar

¼ cup honey

2½ heaping tablespoons brown sugar

1 tablespoon salt

1 cup boiling water

2 cups cold water

¾ cup vegetable oil

2 tablespoons yeast

2½ cups whole wheat flour

5½ cups white flour

Preheat oven to 350°. In mixer bowl, combine, on low speed, the ½ cup flour, sugar, honey, brown sugar, salt, and boiling water. Add in order given: cold water, vegetable oil, yeast, 2½ cups whole wheat, and 5½ cups white flour. When all ingredients have been added, increase speed and mix 9½ minutes. Divide dough into four even portions and shape into loaves. Put into greased bread pans and let rise. Bake approximately 28 minutes. (See color plate 6 for illustration.)

Esther Schlabach, Sarasota, Florida

Lisa's Homemade White Bread

3 cups warm water
3 tablespoons yeast
2 tablespoons salt
½ cup sugar
½ cup oil
½ cup instant or mashed potatoes
8 cups white flour

In large bowl mix water and yeast together. Add salt, sugar, oil, potatoes, and flour. Turn onto floured surface and knead until smooth and elastic; about 10 minutes. Sprinkle more flour on the dough if needed so it's no longer sticky. Grease a large mixing bowl with butter or shortening. Cover with a clean cloth and let rise till double. Punch down and knead; let rise again. Divide dough into 3 parts. Shape into loaves and place in greased bread pans. Let rise until double in size. The second rising takes less time. Bake at 375 for 30 – 35 minutes. Remove bread from pans and let set on cooling racks. Brush tops with butter. Store in plastic bags. Makes 3 loaves. (See color plate 6 for illustration.)

Lisa Miller, Chouteau, Oklahoma

Lemon Poppy Seed Bread

1 box lemon cake mix
1 teaspoon almond extract
1 (3.4 ounce) package lemon or
     vanilla instant pudding
4 eggs
1 cup water
2 tablespoons poppy seeds
¾ cup vegetable oil

Preheat oven to 350°. Combine all ingredients until moistened. Grease and flour bread pan. Bake 20 – 30 minutes until center is done. Also makes good muffins!

Mrs. Matthias (Sarah) Overholt, Sarasota, Florida

1989

Sarasota, Florida

It is now over fifty-two years since we made our first trip to Florida. At that time there were no traffic lights and not many tourists.

In the years 1946 and 1947, we rented at the Becker House on Orange Avenue. The city hall is there now. At the Becker House there were seventy people, Amish and Mennonites. With a hall in the center and bedrooms on either side, we all had to share the same kitchen to cook on the wood-burning stove. The iceman came once a week to fill the large ice box, which held 500 pounds.

One day a woman came in and said she found a Laundromat and we need not wash by hand any longer. It had Maytag wringer washers and two rinse tubs and was located west of Ringling Shopping Center in the city trailer park.

The people of Sarasota said, "If we can get the Mennonites in here, we will have a good community." The city furnished a bus to come right to the Becker House on Sunday to take the people to the Tourist Church.

The next year Jonas Stoltzfus and us bought property right up town. We were the only Amish who owned property uptown. Our first real estate tax was seven cents.

Preacher Enos Yoder, father of Abbie Weaver, built a duplex on Bahia Vista with only the siding boards on and two-by-fours on the inside. The Amish had their own church.

From there Enos built a larger house on Bimini Street where they had Amish church for years. Years later the Amish church people bought a house on Hines Avenue, and it is still being used for Amish church.

Now there are fourteen Mennonite and Amish churches here in Sarasota and Mennonite churches in other parts of Florida.

In the year 1956, we built the first house in Pinecraft with a building permit. This house is on Estrada Street. We had many renters through the years. Les Troyer, who writes "Life Lines" in *The Budget*, was one of our first renters.

C. and Christina Bontrager

Pumpkin Bread

3½ cups flour
3 cups sugar
2 teaspoons baking soda
1½ teaspoons salt
3 teaspoons cinnamon
3 teaspoons nutmeg

½ teaspoon ground ginger
4 eggs
1 cup vegetable oil
⅔ cup water
2 cups canned pumpkin

Preheat oven to 350°. Combine dry ingredients (through ginger) and mix well. Add the 4 moist ingredients. Mix well. Pour into 2 bread pans. Bake 1 hour or until done. This bread freezes really well.

Esther Schlabach, Sarasota, Florida

October 1, 2008
Sunnyside Amish Mennonite Church, Sarasota, Florida

I noticed our little orange trees, planted in March 2007, are heavy laden with fruit already. Temperatures have cooled off some, and with the cooler temperatures comes the anticipation of seeing the Amish buses drive up to the Tourist Church with old friends and new ones. Winter is just around the corner, and with it come folks filling up the park with family reunions, shuffleboard, and volleyball games. There are often evenings of music and singing on Birky Street, and Overholt's Produce will be opening again in November. Yoder's Restaurant has their fall menu up, and everything is coming up pumpkin. The number 16 bus will take you from Bahia Vista Street directly to Siesta Key Beach. Don't fret if you don't have your own three-wheel bike to ride while you're here. You can rent one for just $3 – $4 a day on Kruppa Avenue or from Joe and Mattie on Clarinda Street. Rollerblading is popular with the youth. The roads are freshly paved, and the weather is pleasant. All that's missing is you.

Sherry Gore, Pinecraft, Florida

Banana Sour Cream Bread

¼ cup sugar
1 teaspoon cinnamon
¾ cup butter
3 cups sugar
3 eggs
6 ripe bananas
16 ounces sour cream

2 teaspoons vanilla
2 teaspoons cinnamon
½ teaspoon salt
3 teaspoons baking soda
4½ cups flour
1 cup chopped nuts

Preheat oven to 325°. Grease 4 small or one large loaf pan. In a small bowl, combine ¼ cup sugar and 1 teaspoon cinnamon. Use cinnamon-sugar mixture to dust pan. In large bowl, cream butter, 3 cups sugar, eggs, bananas, sour cream, vanilla, and remaining cinnamon. Mix in salt, baking soda, and flour. Stir in nuts. Bake 1 hour, covering loaves with foil the last 15 minutes of baking time.

Shannon Torkelson, Alberta, Canada

Stuffed Cheese Buns

2 tablespoons yeast
1 cup warm water
2 tablespoons sugar
2 teaspoons garlic powder
¼ cup melted butter
¼ cup olive oil
3 cups flour

2 teaspoons salt
8 ounces mozzarella cheese
Parmesan cheese
3 tablespoons melted butter
½ teaspoon garlic powder
dried parsley flakes

Combine yeast and water and let mixture stand for a couple minutes. Add sugar, garlic powder, melted butter, and oil. Add the flour a little at a time. Add the salt. Knead for at least 10 minutes. Let the dough rise in a greased bowl covered with a wet cloth for about 30 minutes. Preheat oven to 375°. Divide dough into about 20 pieces. Tuck a ¾-inch chunk of cheese in each one and pinch all the edges back up tightly. Place buns pinched side down onto a greased baking sheet. Sprinkle the buns with more shredded cheese and some Parmesan cheese. Bake at 375º 11 – 15 minutes until the bread is golden brown and the cheese is bubbly. Brush with the melted butter and sprinkle with ½ teaspoon garlic powder and parsley flakes. Serve warm. Makes 20 buns.

Sherry Gore, Pinecraft, Florida

Garlic Lover's Cheese Bread

1 loaf French bread (cut into 1-inch slices)	3 tablespoons sour cream
	1 tablespoon dried parsley flakes
1 (8 ounce) package cream cheese	¼ cup Parmesan cheese
6 garlic cloves, minced	2 tablespoons mayonnaise

Setting bread slices aside, beat everything else with mixer until thoroughly blended. Spread each bread slice with mixture and place on baking sheets. Broil for a quick 3 – 4 minutes until golden brown. Makes 10 – 12 servings.

Shannon Torkelson, Alberta, Canada

Monkey Bread

3 tubes buttermilk refrigerated biscuits	1 tablespoon cinnamon
1 cup sugar	1 cup butter
	½ cup brown sugar

Preheat oven to 350°. Open and remove biscuits. Cut each one into 4 pieces. Mix sugar and cinnamon and roll each piece of biscuit into sugar-cinnamon mixture. Place evenly in greased Bundt pan. In small saucepan, melt butter, brown sugar, and a little cinnamon until smooth. Pour over biscuits. Bake 30 minutes or until slightly crunchy on top. Remove from oven and place on plate, upside down, and jiggle until cake falls out. This is a nice treat for the children, when brought to a sister's sewing circle, and extra good when served with hot coffee.

Mrs. Sylvanus (Mary) Hershberger, Millersburg, Ohio

Aunt Mary's Corn Bread

margarine or bacon grease
1 cup self-rising cornmeal
1 small can creamed corn
2 tablespoons sugar

1 cup sour cream
3 teaspoons baking powder
¼ cup vegetable oil
2 eggs, beaten

Preheat oven to 425°. Let margarine or bacon grease melt in baking dish while oven heats. Mix ingredients well. Pour into hot, greased 7x11-inch pan and bake 15 minutes or until golden brown and crusty.

Miriam Good, Elida, Ohio

Premium Gingerbread
with Old-Fashioned Lemon Sauce

1 egg
1½ teaspoons baking soda
½ cup butter
½ teaspoon nutmeg
½ cup sugar
½ teaspoon cinnamon

1 cup molasses
½ teaspoon ginger
2½ cups flour
1½ teaspoons baking powder
⅞ cup boiling water (1 cup minus
    2 tablespoons)

Old-Fashioned Lemon Sauce

1 cup sugar
1 egg, well beaten
¼ cup butter

¾ teaspoon grated lemon zest
¼ cup water
3 tablespoons lemon juice

Premium Gingerbread: Preheat oven to 350°. Mix all ingredients, adding water last. Bake 35 minutes. Serve with lemon sauce and whipped topping. *Old-Fashioned Lemon Sauce:* Mix all ingredients in 2-quart saucepan. Heat to boiling over medium heat, stirring constantly. Refrigerate any remaining sauce.

Wilma Lee Yoder, Sarasota, Florida

Butter Horns

1 tablespoon yeast	½ teaspoon salt
1 teaspoon white sugar	½ cup butter, melted
1 cup lukewarm water	3 eggs, beaten
½ cup white sugar	4½ cups flour

Dissolve yeast with 1 teaspoon sugar in warm water. Let set and rise a little. Combine sugar, salt, butter, and eggs. Add yeast mixture. Mix well. Add flour. Cover and let rise in refrigerator overnight. Divide dough in 3 parts. Roll each part into 12-inch circle. Cut into 8 wedges. Roll each piece from wide end to narrow. Place on greased baking sheets. Let rise. Preheat oven to 350°. Bake 12 – 15 minutes. Brush with melted butter. If I'm in a hurry, I make it all the same day. Makes 24.

Mrs. Fremon (Sarah) Miller, Walnut Creek, Ohio

Pizza Crust

¼ cup vegetable oil	1 tablespoon yeast, heaping
1 egg	½ cup warm water
2 tablespoons sugar	3 – 3½ cups flour
½ cup hot water	cheese
1 teaspoon salt	favorite toppings

Preheat oven to 400°. Combine vegetable oil and egg. Add sugar, hot water, and salt. Dissolve yeast in warm water, then add to first mixture. Mix in flour. Knead 15 minutes and let rise 1 hour. Roll onto large pan (jelly roll pan works great), spread with sauce, and bake 20 minutes. Next add cheese, your favorite toppings, more cheese, and finish baking until cheese is melted. This is a very delicious, soft crust.

Regina (Byler) Stutzman, Sarasota, Florida

Whole-Wheat Pizza Dough

1½ tablespoons yeast
1⅛ cups warm water
3 cups whole-wheat flour

¾ teaspoon salt
1½ tablespoons sugar
½ cup vegetable oil

Preheat oven to 350°. Dissolve yeast in warm water with sugar. Stir in remaining ingredients. Let rise 30–40 minutes. Spread in 2 ungreased pizza pans or 1 large sheet pan. Bake 10 minutes. Add toppings of your choice. Bake 15 minutes more.

Sarah Joy Beiler, Pinecraft, Florida

March 28, 2007
Sunnyside Amish Mennonite Church, Sarasota, Florida

The schoolteachers and students are preparing for science and art night coming up on Friday. Teacher Sarah Mohler held Pioneer Day for her class recently, and the children came to school dressed in 1800s-era clothing. They made moccasins and learned how to hand-dip candles. Some of their work was done outside, as was that of Rosita's class and Mel's and Ann's too — only not by choice. One boy (who shall remain nameless lest he glory in his fame) overcooked and blew up a hot dog in the microwave, resulting in what looked like a prehistoric piece of charcoal, bowl included. The black smoke was thick enough to evacuate the school for a time, keeping Rosita's class out of doors for the remainder of the day. I had a hard time keeping a straight face as I drove to the schoolhouse to pick up that boy and bring him home, as he was dismissed for the remainder of the day.

Sherry Gore, Pinecraft, Florida

Dutch Dinner Rolls

2 cups warm milk	4 eggs, beaten
2 teaspoons salt	2 tablespoons yeast
1 cup warm water	3 pounds 4 ounces high-gluten
½ cup sugar	flour (about 10¼ cups)
¾ cup margarine	

Combine all ingredients to form dough and let rise. Punch down and let rise again until double in bulk. Punch down and shape into small balls. Put in pan and let rise until almost double. Bake at 325° 15–20 minutes. Dough will be sticky, so you will need to grease or spray your hands with nonstick cooking spray. Rolls will be too dry if you add more flour. Very good. Makes 36–42 dinner rolls. (See color plate 12 for illustration.)

Mrs. Samuel (Irma) Bender, Sarasota, Florida

Dampf Knepp

This is a quick and easy dessert that Grosmommy (grandmother) used to make when she had bread dough rising.

brown sugar	cream
bread dough	milk

Preheat oven to 350°. Grease an iron skillet and cover the bottom with brown sugar. Shape dough into little buns and place on top of sugar. Let rise half an hour. Pour enough cream over the top to make a good sauce with the brown sugar. Bake until light and golden in color. Serve warm with milk. They can also be eaten cold.

Sam and Katie Yoder, Rose Hill, Virginia

Mrs. Byler's Glazed Doughnuts

2 cups mashed potatoes	3 packages dry yeast
½ cup butter	¾ cup lukewarm water
½ cup margarine	3 cups flour
1 cup sugar	2 eggs, beaten
1 quart whole milk, scalded	1 tablespoon salt

Combine mashed potatoes, butter, margarine, and sugar. Add scalded milk. Dissolve yeast in lukewarm water. When yeast has begun to work, add to mashed potato mixture. Add half the flour and let set until it sponges. Add eggs and salt, then add remainder of flour and mix well. Let set until double in bulk. Roll out and cut out donuts. Let set again until double in bulk. Fry in hot shortening at 375° until golden brown.

Sherry Gore, Pinecraft, Florida

Glaze Recipe

8 cups powdered sugar	1 tablespoon vanilla
¼ cup butter	1 cup milk
¼ cup margarine	

Combine all ingredients. Drop donuts into glaze while still hot and place on wire or stick until dry.

Vera Kipfer, Pinecraft, Florida

Cake Doughnuts

2 eggs	¼ teaspoon nutmeg
1 cup sugar	¼ teaspoon cinnamon
2 tablespoons shortening	4 teaspoons baking powder
3½ cups flour, sifted	¾ cup milk
½ teaspoon salt	

Beat eggs and add sugar and shortening. Cream well. Stir in rest of ingredients. Turn onto floured board and knead 5 or 6 times. Roll out

⅓-inch thick. Let dough rest 20 minutes. Cut with floured doughnut cutter. Deep fry in cooking oil. Turn doughnuts when they rise to the top, and cook until brown. Carefully remove from oil and place on paper towels. Doughnuts are delicious plain or can be shaken in paper bag of powdered sugar or cinnamon and powdered sugar mixture. Makes 2 dozen.

Laura Yoder, Sarasota, Florida

Ever-Ready Raisin Bran Muffins

15 ounce box of raisin bran cereal
5 cups flour
3 cups sugar
5 teaspoons soda
2 teaspoons salt

1 cup vegetable oil
4 eggs, beaten
4 cups buttermilk
2 teaspoons vanilla

Preheat oven to 375°. Combine dry ingredients. Add remaining ingredients. Mix well with spoon. Bake in muffin pans 12 – 15 minutes. Batter keeps in refrigerator for up to 6 weeks. Makes approximately 50 muffins.

Ann Mast, Sarasota, Florida

Morning Glory Muffins

2½ cups flour
1¼ cups sugar
3 teaspoons cinnamon
2 teaspoons baking soda
½ teaspoon salt
3 eggs
¾ cup applesauce
½ cup vegetable oil

1 teaspoon vanilla
2 cups grated carrots
1 medium tart apple, peeled
    and grated
1 (8 ounce) can crushed pineapple
½ cup flaked coconut
½ cup raisins
½ cup chopped walnuts

Preheat oven to 350°. In a large bowl, combine the first 5 ingredients (through salt). In another bowl combine eggs, applesauce, vegetable oil, and vanilla. Stir into dry ingredients just until moistened (batter will be thick). Stir in rest of ingredients. Fill paper-lined muffin cups two-thirds full. Bake 20 – 24 minutes or until toothpick comes out clean. Cool 5 minutes before removing from pans. Makes 2 dozen.

Mrs. Sam (Katie) Yoder, Rose Hill, Virginia

Cranberry Surprise Muffins

2 cups flour	2 eggs
2 tablespoons sugar	1 cup milk
3 teaspoons baking powder	¼ cup butter, melted
½ teaspoon salt	1 cup jellied cranberry sauce

Preheat oven to 400°. Combine dry ingredients in a bowl. Whisk together eggs, milk, and butter. Add cranberry sauce. Stir together until moistened. Put in muffin tins sprayed with nonstick cooking spray. Bake 12 – 15 minutes.

Sadie Hochstetler, Sarasota, Florida

Cranberry Orange Bread

1 cup fresh cranberries, chopped	¾ teaspoon salt
½ cup sugar	1 egg, beaten
1 teaspoon grated orange zest	¼ cup orange juice
1¾ cups flour	½ cup milk
2½ teaspoons baking powder	⅓ cup vegetable oil

Preheat oven to 400°. Mix cranberries, sugar, and orange zest. Set aside. Sift together flour, baking powder, and salt in large bowl. In separate bowl, combine egg, orange juice, milk, and cooking oil. Add to dry ingredients, stirring until just moistened. Fold in cranberry mixture. Put in bread pan and bake 30 – 35 minutes or until done. Serve warm.

Mrs. Perry (Susan) Miller, Sarasota, Florida

Blueberry Streusel Muffins

½ cup sugar
½ cup butter, softened
1 egg, beaten
2⅓ cups flour
4 teaspoons baking powder

½ teaspoon salt
1 cup milk
1 teaspoon vanilla
1½ cups blueberries, fresh
    or frozen

Streusel

½ cup sugar
⅓ cup flour

½ teaspoon cinnamon
¼ cup butter

Muffins: Preheat oven to 350°. Cream sugar and butter. Add egg and mix well. Combine flour, baking powder, and salt. Add to creamed mixture alternating with milk. Stir in vanilla. Gently fold in blueberries. Fill 12 paper-lined muffin cups. *Streusel:* In small bowl, combine sugar, flour, and cinnamon. Cut in butter until crumbly. Sprinkle over muffins. Bake 25 – 30 minutes.

Mrs. Larry (Kathy) Byler, Pinecraft, Florida

Mile-High Biscuits

3 cups sifted flour
¾ teaspoon salt
4½ teaspoons baking powder
¾ teaspoon cream of tartar

2½ tablespoons sugar
¾ cup shortening
1 egg
1 cup milk

Preheat oven to 450°. Sift dry ingredients. Cut in shortening until crumbly. Beat egg lightly; add to milk. Combine liquid with dry ingredients using fork. Roll 1 inch thick. Cut out and place on greased cookie sheets. Bake 12 minutes. Makes 2 dozen.

Barbara Yoder, Sarasota, Florida

FLOUR

If a recipe calls for 1 cup sifted flour, working over a piece of waxed paper, sift the flour directly into a measuring cup and level the flour with a knife.

Self-rising flour is all-purpose flour that has baking powder mixed in. Make your own by adding 1¼ teaspoons baking powder and a pinch of salt to 1 cup all-purpose flour.

TIP

Pastry flour makes great pie dough, cookies, doughnuts, and muffins. To make your own pastry flour, combine 1⅓ cups all-purpose flour with ⅔ cup cake flour.

All-purpose flour is half cake flour and half bread flour. It makes a great flour for perfect pizza, cakes, and most all baking.

Cake flour has less gluten than all other wheat flours and is used in recipes calling for light cakes, such as sponge cake. Make your own by substituting 1¾ cups all-purpose flour and ¼ cup cornstarch. Or you can substitute all-purpose flour for cake flour by using 1 cup minus 2 tablespoons all-purpose flour.

Whole-wheat flour is brown and is derived from 100 percent of the wheat berry (the bran and germ). It has a nutty flavor and a denser texture than all-purpose flour. When completely substituting whole-wheat flour for white, use ⅞ cup whole wheat for 1 cup white flour. For best results, store whole-wheat flour in the refrigerator or freezer.

*Christians may not see eye to eye,
but we can walk arm in arm.*
Willis Bontrager

October 3, 2007
Sunnyside Amish Mennonite Church, Sarasota, Florida

The youth held their first youth mission fundraiser by serving a delicious meal they prepared themselves. Lasagna, breadsticks, and salad were on the menu, as was homemade ice cream brought by Brenda's father, Lee Keim. The youth are raising money to go on their mission trip. With such an age gap between them, the older unmarrieds in their late twenties no longer attend the youth meetings, though they do come to youth Sunday school class. Nathan Overholt was voted in recently as teacher for the third year in a row.

Sherry Gore, Pinecraft, Florida

Parmesan Pan Bread

2 cups warm water
1 tablespoon yeast
1 teaspoon salt
1 tablespoon vegetable oil

1 teaspoon sugar
2¾ cups flour
¼ cup Italian dressing

Topping

1 cup shredded mozzarella cheese
¼ cup Parmesan cheese
dash pepper
¼ teaspoon Italian seasoning

½ teaspoon garlic salt
¼ teaspoon dried oregano
dash basil

Preheat oven to 450°. Combine bread ingredients thoroughly with mixer and let rise 15 minutes. Spread in 13x9-inch pan; cover with Italian dressing. Mix topping ingredients and sprinkle over bread. Bake 15 minutes. Eat with sauce of your choice.

Regina Yoder, Summertown, Tennessee

Cinnamon Rolls

⅔ cup sugar

1 cup warm water

2 packages yeast

2 teaspoons sugar

1 teaspoon salt

1 cup mashed potatoes

4 eggs, beaten

6 cups flour

⅔ cup vegetable oil

Filling

soft butter

brown sugar

cinnamon

Preheat oven to 350°. Combine sugar, water, and yeast. Add the rest of roll ingredients and mix well. Let dough rise until double. Break into two portions. Roll out dough one portion at a time and spread with soft butter, brown sugar, and cinnamon. Roll up from long side and cut into 1¾-inch slices. Place in pan. Let rise and bake until brown, about 15 – 20 minutes.

Mrs. Dan (Martha) Stutzman, Pinecraft, Florida

October 21, 2009
Sunnyside Amish Mennonite Church, Sarasota, Florida

Yesterday was the start of a new Sunday school term. This was my first time teaching the primary class. I wondered afterward if the children enjoyed the class. Isaiah's mother, Mrs. Jason (Angi) Gingerich, shared this: "I've just got to tell you this, Sherry. Isaiah was pretty nervous of starting a new class, so I asked him this afternoon, 'How did you like your Sunday school class?' 'I love Miss Sherry! She's the best teacher ever!' he gushed." I immediately felt tears well up in my eyes, and she continued, "'Was it because of cinnamon rolls?' He said, 'Yeah, that helped.'"

Sherry Gore, Pinecraft, Florida

Cappuccino Muffins

2 cups flour
¾ cup sugar
2½ teaspoons baking powder
1 teaspoon cinnamon
½ teaspoon salt
1 cup milk

2 tablespoons instant coffee
½ cup butter
1 egg, beaten
1 teaspoon vanilla extract
¾ cup miniature chocolate chips

Espresso Spread

4 ounces cream cheese, cubed
½ teaspoon instant coffee
1 tablespoon sugar

½ teaspoon vanilla extract
¼ cup miniature chocolate chips

Preheat oven to 350°. In a bowl, combine flour, sugar, baking powder, cinnamon, and salt. In separate bowl, stir milk and coffee granules until coffee is dissolved. Add butter, egg, and vanilla. Mix well. Stir into dry ingredients just until moistened. Fold in chocolate chips. Fill greased or paper-lined muffin cups two-thirds full. Bake 17 – 20 minutes. Meanwhile combine Espresso Spread ingredients in a small bowl. Remove muffins from pan as soon as they are removed from oven and frost immediately to melt chocolate. Makes about 14 muffins.

Sherry Gore, Pinecraft, Florida

Lisa's Brown Bread

1½ cups boiling water
1 cup old-fashioned oats
2 tablespoons shortening
2 teaspoons salt
1 package yeast
¾ cup warm water

½ teaspoon sugar
¼ cup brown sugar
¼ cup molasses
4¾ – 5½ cups flour
butter, melted

Heat oven to 375°. Combine boiling water, oats, shortening, and salt. Cool. In large bowl, dissolve yeast in warm water. Sprinkle with sugar. Add oat mixture, brown sugar, molasses, and 3 cups flour; mix well. Add enough remaining flour to form soft dough. Turn onto floured surface; knead until smooth. Place in greased bowl; cover and let rise. Divide and place in greased bread pans. Bake 30 – 35 minutes or until golden brown. Brush with melted butter. Makes 2 loaves.

Keep brown sugar soft by storing with two large marshmallows in an airtight container.

TIP

Lisa Miller, Chouteau, Oklahoma

Breakfast

Dippy Eggs

It doesn't take much to embarrass a teenage boy. On a hunting trip to Kentucky, while ordering breakfast, son Tyler forgot he was out of town and instantly regretted telling the waitress, "I'll have two dippy eggs, please."

Break eggs one at a time into the same heated skillet you fried bacon in. Do not stir or turn eggs. Spoon bacon grease over eggs as they cook for about 3 – 4 minutes. (See color plate 8 for illustration.)

Sherry Gore, Pinecraft, Florida

Granola

4 cups rolled oats

1 cup coconut flakes

1 cup brown sugar

1 teaspoon cinnamon

¾ cup cooking oil

½ teaspoon salt

2 teaspoons vanilla

Preheat oven to 325°. Combine the first four ingredients (through cinnamon). Pour into shallow baking pans. Combine cooking oil, salt, and vanilla. Pour over dry mixture. Bake 45 minutes, stirring often.

Mrs. Noah (Lucy) Gingerich, Holmes County, Ohio

Baked Oatmeal

This makes a perfect dish when chilly weather arrives.

½ cup vegetable oil

½ cup flaked coconut

½ cup honey

1 teaspoon salt

1 cup milk

1½ teaspoons baking soda

2 eggs, beaten

1 teaspoon vanilla

3 cups oats

½ cup nuts and ½ cup raisins
   (optional)

Preheat oven to 325°. Mix all together and bake in 13x9-inch cake pan 25 – 30 minutes. Eat warm or cold with milk. Makes 10 – 12 servings.

Vera Overholt, Pinecraft, Florida

Plump Pumpkin Pancakes

1 cup flour

2 tablespoons sugar

pinch baking soda

⅛ teaspoon nutmeg

¼ teaspoon cinnamon

⅛ teaspoon ginger

1 egg, beaten

1¼ cups milk

2 tablespoons shortening, melted

½ cup canned pumpkin

maple syrup (optional)

Combine flour, sugar, baking soda, and spices in small bowl. In large bowl, combine wet ingredients; add to flour mixture. Beat until smooth. Bake on hot (350°), lightly greased skillet. Turn when edges begin to bubble. Enjoy with maple syrup.

Shannon Torkelson, Alberta, Canada

Stuffed Raspberry French Toast

8 slices bread	butter
8 ounces cream cheese	1 cup raspberry jam or puree
1 tablespoon milk per egg	powdered sugar
eggs, beaten	maple syrup (optional)

Spread cream cheese on 2 slices bread; sandwich together. Dip sandwich into eggs and fry in buttered skillet. Brown on both sides. Pour raspberries over top and sprinkle with powdered sugar. May be eaten with maple syrup. (See color plate 2 for illustration.)

Sherry Gore, Pinecraft, Florida

Gingerbread Waffles

These make a delicious treat slathered in butter and topped with a dollop of whipped topping on Christmas morning. Makes 6 large waffles.

2 cups all-purpose flour	2 eggs, separated
3 teaspoons baking powder	1½ cups buttermilk
2 teaspoons ground ginger	½ cup molasses
1½ teaspoons ground cinnamon	¼ cup plus 2 tablespoons butter, melted
1 teaspoon ground allspice	
1 teaspoons baking soda	⅔ cup raisins (optional)
½ teaspoon salt	¼ teaspoon cream of tartar
⅔ cup packed brown sugar	

In a bowl, combine flour, baking powder, ginger, cinnamon, allspice, baking soda, and salt; set aside. In a large mixing bowl, beat brown sugar and egg yolk until fluffy. Add milk, molasses, and butter; stir into dry ingredients until combined. Do not overbeat. Add raisins. In a small bowl, beat egg white and cream of tartar until soft peaks form. Gently fold into batter. Bake in a preheated waffle iron sprayed with nonstick cooking spray. Delicious when served hot, slathered in butter, and with a light dusting of powdered sugar and warmed maple syrup poured over top. (See color plate 4 for illustration.)

Sherry Gore, Pinecraft, Florida

Breakfast Casserole

The first I remember this recipe was while I lived at Aylmer, Ontario. When we had company overnight, we would fix the casserole in the evening, and in the morning we'd pop it in the wood-burning kitchen stove. By the time the house warmed up and everybody was out of bed, breakfast was on the table.

Katie Troyer, Pinecraft, Florida

1 pound sausage or ham	1 teaspoon dry mustard
6 eggs	1 cup grated cheese
2 cups milk	8 – 10 bread slices
1 teaspoon salt	

Preheat oven to 350°. Brown sausage, crumble, and drain fat. Beat eggs with milk, salt, and mustard. Layer sausage, bread, and cheese in baking dish. Pour mixture over top. May be refrigerated overnight. Bake 45 minutes.

Mary Stoltzfus, Cleveland, North Carolina

Coffee Soup

Bishop Bill Yoder says an Amish cookbook isn't complete without a recipe for Coffee Soup.

2 slices bread	½ cup half-and-half
1 cup hot coffee	1 – 2 tablespoons sugar

Break the bread into bite-size pieces. Combine the coffee, half-and-half, and sugar. Place the bread cubes in a soup bowl and pour the coffee mixture over all. Sprinkle extra sugar or cinnamon sugar over top.

Sherry Gore, Pinecraft, Florida

Florida Avocado Egg Scramble

1 avocado	½ cup sour cream
salt	1 teaspoon pepper
8 eggs	1 tablespoon butter

Cut avocado lengthwise into halves. Remove and discard skin and pit. Dice avocado and sprinkle with salt. Beat eggs with sour cream. Season with salt and pepper. Melt butter in skillet. Add egg mixture and cook on medium-low heat, stirring occasionally. When almost set, gently fold in avocado. Makes 4 servings.

Sherry Gore, Pinecraft, Florida

Cheesy Egg Puffs

I prepared these tasty egg puffs while hosting the 10th annual cooking show at Das Dutchman Essenhaus in Middlebury, Indiana.

1 tablespoon butter	½ cup butter, melted
½ pound fresh mushrooms, sliced	10 eggs, lightly beaten
4 green onions, chopped	4 cups shredded Monterey Jack
½ cup flour	cheese
1 teaspoon baking powder	2 cups small curd cottage cheese
½ teaspoon salt	

Preheat oven to 350°. Sauté 1 tablespoon butter, fresh mushrooms, and green onions in skillet until tender. Combine with ½ cup flour, baking powder, and salt. In another bowl combine ½ cup butter, eggs, shredded cheese, and cottage cheese. Stir all together in large bowl. Fill greased muffin cups three-quarters full. Bake 35 minutes. Makes 2½ dozen.

Sherry Gore, Pinecraft, Florida

June 18, 2008
Sunnyside Amish Mennonite Church, Sarasota, Florida

I made a mistake two weeks ago that I would come to regret later. Son Tyler left a feeder mouse in my van that was bought for his yucky snake. Tyler came into the house proclaiming to his sisters, "There's a mouse loose in the van! You should have heard Mom; she screamed like a teapot!" It managed to survive the heat and has been living off a bag of spilled M&M's.

Good things are going on at Yoder's Restaurant! Sledgehammers and axes were put to use this week, as workers are busy transforming the little building by the bike rack into an Amish gift shop, which the owners plan to open in time for the winter crowd. Fresh strawberry pie is on the menu, making for some long lines at the door. Across the street, Abigail Overholt has been making some changes and had some outdoor furniture delivered to accommodate customers in her hope of opening their produce stand earlier than usual.

Over the years, Matthias Overholt has kept us waiting and wondering if he was ever going to find the right girl. A trip to Washington State to meet the family of one such young lady provided the answer. He was so happy upon his return to Sarasota, it made you wonder if he needed that plane to return home, for he was flying on cloud nine when he shared his news with us. It is teacher Sarah Mohler who has captured his heart. She's an exceptional person who brightens the way wherever she goes.

Needing to run up the road to CVS pharmacy in Pinecraft, I went in my housecoat, thinking, *Why not? It's only eight-tenths of a mile from home. What could happen between here and there?* Jacinda went in the store while I waited in the van. It was then the little white fugitive with the beady red eyes suddenly made his appearance. To my horror, it was my bare feet he ran across! I grabbed the door handle to jump out. Seeing the sleeve of my housecoat brought me to the horrid realization that I was not getting out of the van. The parking lot was crowded, as Mom's Amish Restaurant was closing for the night. Waitress Eleanor (Wilmer) Miller walked out the door and came over to see what the fuss was. She was unimpressed with the situation and said, "Oh, let me get him. I can catch him. I'm not afraid." I told her no, he was too fast. She bravely insisted on having a look. "Fine," I said. "Open the back door and have a try." I turned around just as she had the door open, and saw the mouse run up the backseat. Then I heard that familiar sound — the teapot scream — only it wasn't me this time; it was Eleanor!

Sherry Gore, Pinecraft, Florida

Corn Mush with Tomato Gravy

Dad was gone when we were growing up, so it was Mom's job to stretch the budget. With six children at home, this wasn't easy. She would often make tomato gravy for our breakfast.

Minister Jason Gingerich, son of Bishop
Lester Gingerich, Sarasota, Florida

1 cup cold water	3 cups boiling water
1 cup cornmeal	1 teaspoon salt

Mix cold water and cornmeal together in bowl. Stir into pot of boiling water and add salt. Cook, stirring until it starts to boil again. Cook on low heat 30 – 45 minutes. Pour into loaf pan or deep glass baking dish. Chill overnight. Will set firm. In the morning, when you're good and hungry, cut slices ½- inch thick. Tempting as it seems, don't take a bite yet. After adding oil to a hot skillet, fry corn mush until golden brown on both sides. Either pour maple syrup on top or eat with your favorite tomato gravy, depending on what you're in the mood for. Eat and enjoy! (See color plate 8 for illustration.)

Sherry Gore, Pinecraft, Florida

Tomato Gravy

2 tablespoons flour	4 cups tomato juice
1 cup milk	salt and pepper to taste

Bring tomato juice to a boil in a pot. Mix together flour and milk in jar and shake. Add to boiling tomato juice. Bring to a boil a second time and remove from heat. Add salt and pepper to taste. Pour over your corn meal mush and dig in!

Sherry Gore, Pinecraft, Florida

Sunshine Baked Eggs

1 pound bacon, fried	1 can crushed pineapple
14 eggs	1 teaspoon vanilla
1½ cups cottage cheese	chopped fresh parsley

Preheat oven to 350°. Fry bacon until crisp; save 2 tablespoons drippings. Crumble bacon; beat eggs lightly; add saved drippings, cottage cheese, pineapple, and vanilla. Put in 7x11-inch casserole dish. Top with parsley. Bake uncovered 40 – 45 minutes. Makes 12 servings.

Mrs. Dan Hochstetler, Topeka, Indiana

Katie Ann's Breakfast Gravy

1 large onion	¼ teaspoon pepper
4 tablespoons butter	1½ teaspoons salt
3 cups milk	6 tablespoons flour
1 teaspoon dry mustard	12 hard-boiled eggs, diced
2 teaspoons vinegar	

Fry onion in butter (do not brown). Mix milk, mustard, vinegar, pepper, salt, and flour in blender. Heat until thickened. Add onion mixture and eggs. Serve over toast or biscuits. Makes 6 cups.

Martha Hostetler, Pinecraft, Florida

Potato Crawlers

2¾ cups flour
¾ cup sugar
4 tablespoons baking powder
1 teaspoon cinnamon
¼ teaspoon nutmeg
3 tablespoons shortening

3 eggs
1 cup mashed potatoes
   (leftover is fine)
1 teaspoon vanilla
½ cup milk

Mix all ingredients together well. Dropping by rounded teaspoonfuls, deep fry at 365° until golden brown. Roll in powdered or granulated sugar or glaze.

Glaze

½ tablespoon unflavored gelatin
⅛ cup cold water
¼ cup boiling water

¾ pound (scant 3 cups) powdered
   sugar
½ tablespoon butter
½ teaspoon vanilla

Soften gelatin in cold water; dissolve in boiling water. Add sugar, butter and vanilla. This glaze does not get sticky and stays on even after freezing. Can be used for donuts also.

Mrs. John Henry (Minnie) Schmucker, Burkesville, Kentucky

Sausage Gravy

1 pound sage-seasoned sausage
1 cup flour
10 cups whole milk

2 teaspoons salt
½ teaspoon pepper or more
   to taste

Brown sausage in large saucepan over medium heat until cooked through and crumbled. Remove sausage from pan and set aside. Add flour to drippings and stir quickly. Add milk, salt, and pepper; stir. More or less milk may be added, depending on how thick you like your gravy. Add sausage crumbles. Continue cooking over low heat 15 minutes. Makes 3 quarts.

Sherry Gore, Pinecraft, Florida

Farmer's Skillet

6 strips bacon, chopped
2 tablespoons finely chopped onion
3 cooked potatoes, cubed

6 eggs, beaten
2 tablespoons milk
salt and pepper to taste
½ cup cheddar cheese, shredded

In a heavy skillet, cook bacon until crisp; remove to paper towels to drain. In drippings, cook onion and potatoes until browned, about 5 minutes. Pour beaten eggs and milk into skillet. Cook, stirring gently, until eggs are set. Season with salt and pepper; sprinkle with the bacon and cheese. Makes 4 servings.

Sherry Gore, Pinecraft, Florida

Country Caramel French Toast

Wake up to a gourmet breakfast, without the fuss!

1 cup brown sugar
½ cup butter
2 tablespoons light corn syrup
12 slices white bread
¼ cup sugar

1 teaspoon cinnamon, divided
6 eggs, beaten
1½ cups milk
1 teaspoon vanilla

Preheat oven to 350°. Lightly grease 13x9-inch baking dish; set aside. Bring brown sugar, butter, and corn syrup to a boil. Remove from heat; pour into baking dish. Top with 6 slices bread; sprinkle with combined sugar and ½ teaspoon cinnamon. Top with remaining bread. Beat eggs, milk, vanilla, and remaining cinnamon; pour over bread. Cover and refrigerate overnight. Remove dish from refrigerator. Bake 30 – 35 minutes. Makes 8 servings.

Sherry Gore, Pinecraft, Florida

Thomas Peachy, also known as the "Flying Dutchman," sustained severe injuries when the rear axle of his three-wheel motorbike broke. He was wise in having a heavy-duty axle installed, as his bike is powered by a fast motor to help him with the long trek to the new Big Olaf creamery, where he churns ice cream. Thomas, a minister of the Amish Church, was coasting back into Pinecraft, traveling about 20 mph when the axle broke, causing him to lose control of the bike. This forced him and the bike into oncoming traffic on Bahia Vista Street. According to Thomas, a car lightly hit him, causing him to be thrown. Later it was determined his leg had been run over. He says he has another bike to use, only it's slower. "Sherry, you'll have to change my name now," he said.

"Yes, Thomas," I replied. "We'll call you the 'Pedaling Dutchman.'"

Dutch Blueberry Babies

This makes a spectacular dish. Set the cast iron skillet in the middle of the table for company and expect applause!

¼ cup butter	⅛ teaspoon cinnamon
1½ cups milk	8 eggs
1½ cups flour	blueberries, frozen or fresh
¾ teaspoon salt	sugar
¾ teaspoon nutmeg	

Put butter in the center of a cast iron skillet. Place pan in oven preheated to 425°. Whisk together the milk, flour, salt, nutmeg, and cinnamon until smooth. Add the eggs and whisk until fully combined. Once the oven is hot and the butter in the pan is completely melted, remove the pan and swirl the butter around to coat all surfaces. Add blueberries. Pour batter evenly over the blueberries. Bake 20 – 30 minutes, until center is cooked through. Dust generously with powdered sugar. (See color plate 31 for illustration.)

Nancy Good, Sarasota, Florida

Appetizers and Beverages

Homemade Barbecue Sauce

2 cups ketchup
½ teaspoon garlic powder
½ cup brown sugar

½ cup chopped onion
1 teaspoon Liquid Smoke

Combine sauce ingredients in blender and store in refrigerator. Keeps well for a month or more. Delicious with meatballs and anything you are barbecuing. Makes 2½ cups.

Sara Ann Petersheim, Lancaster, Pennsylvania

Baste for Barbecuing Chicken

½ cup vinegar (scant)
2 teaspoons garlic powder
1 quart water

2 tablespoons Worcestershire
  sauce
4 tablespoons salt

Make enough baste to cover raw chicken. Marinate overnight in refrigerator. Makes 4½ cups.

Mrs. Joe (Mattie) Yoder, Colon, Michigan

January 18, 2006
3445 Birky Street, Sarasota, Florida

Twenty years ago we opened a savings account with a bank on Main Street in downtown Sarasota. Others from Pinecraft banked there too.

Then Milt Yoder built a building on the northeast corner of Kaufman and Bahia Vista in Pinecraft and a bank moved in. Because it was within walking distance, we soon changed. One of the first tellers was Janet (Barkman) Stutzman, a young lady with a pleasant personality who did not hesitate to talk Pennsylvania Dutch if an Amish customer came in. But after a number of years, it closed because there were two other branches nearby.

In July 2005 Mennonite Financial Federal Credit moved in. They don't call it a bank, but they do everything a bank does. For $25 you can become a member, and you are ready to do business. We opened an account with them this week. I liked everything I saw. Their brochure read, "Financial services for Mennonites, Amish, Brethren in Christ, and other Anabaptists." The main office is in Lancaster, Pennsylvania. There is one in Kidron, Ohio, and now one here in Sarasota.

The pavilion at the Pinecraft Park is finished and got its first tryout last evening, Friday the thirteenth. Barbecued chicken with a meal was carry-out or eat there. This was for a donation, and the proceeds will go for expenses of the upcoming Haiti benefit auction in February.

Noah Gingerich

Fruit Dip

½ cup sugar

1 egg, beaten

2 tablespoons pineapple juice

4 ounces cream cheese

1 cup nondairy whipped topping

Cook sugar, egg, and pineapple juice together until thick. Add cream cheese. When cool, add whipped topping and beat well. Makes about 2½ cups. (See color plate 1 for illustration.)

Mrs. Sam (Martha) Hostetler, Pinecraft, Florida

Iced Coffee

½ cup sugar

1½ tablespoons instant coffee

1½ cups brewed coffee

½ teaspoon vanilla

Combine ingredients in 2-quart pitcher. Add milk until half full. Add ice until full. Makes 1 gallon.

Kathleen Schlabach, Sarasota, Florida

Quick Homemade Root Beer

2 cups sugar

4 teaspoons yeast

4 teaspoons root beer extract

Pour all into a gallon jug. Fill about half full of lukewarm water. Shake until sugar is dissolved. Fill jug with lukewarm water. Cap tightly. Set in sun 4 hours. Chill overnight. Ready to serve. This is especially good when ice cream is added to make a Homemade Root Beer Float. (See color plate 3 for illustration.)

Mrs. Mervin (Fannie Kay) Yoder, Chouteau, Oklahoma

Sarah Joy's Tea

1 gallon-size tea bag or 4 family-size or 9 cup-size tea bags

1 quart boiling water
1½ cups sugar

Brew tea 20 minutes. Add sugar. Pour over water or ice in gallon jar. Serve with lemon or lime wedges. Makes 1 gallon.

Sarah Joy Beiler, Pinecraft, Florida

November 9, 2009
Sunnyside Amish Mennonite Church, Sarasota, Florida

Daughter Shannon and I were walking up to the door of the fellowship hall Friday evening when she looked at me and said, "I didn't know they were having a singing." They weren't. It was Lester Hostetler, sitting in as auctioneer for the night. The youth brought in a little over $2,000 that night serving piña colada – flavored smoothies and iced coffee. Most of the funds raised came from services auctioned off to the highest bidders. Among those offered were sewing, baking, cleaning, car repair, lawn work, a Dominican dinner for six to eight people prepared by Kris and Rebecca Knepp, and a four-hour water-skiing excursion by Tim Gingerich.

Sherry Gore, Pinecraft, Florida

It really is a blast in Pinecraft,
especially if you're Amish.
Kevin Williams

Southern Breeze Punch

1 envelope blue raspberry
  Kool-Aid
1 (6 ounce) can frozen lemonade
  concentrate
1 cup sugar
7 cups water
2 liters ginger ale
1 (46 ounce) can pineapple juice

Mix all ingredients. Fill each glass with ice cubes and pour punch mixture over them to fill glass. Stir briskly and allow a few minutes for the cubes to thaw into the punch. This is a very refreshing drink and not too sweet. Keep some ice cubes in the freezer, then you can quickly mix up a refreshing drink to serve your guests. Makes 1½ gallons plus ice. (See color plate 1 for illustration.)

Esther Schlabach, Sarasota, Florida

Slushy Punch

1 (6 ounce) package orange Jell-O
2 cups sugar
1 quart boiling water
2 quarts cold water
1 (46 ounce) can pineapple juice
lemon-lime soda

Dissolve Jell-O and sugar in boiling water; add cold water and pineapple juice. Freeze. Should be frozen until slushy. When ready to serve, fill a glass ¾ full with slush and pour lemon-lime soda over it. Makes 1½ gallons.

Mrs. Mervin (Fannie Kay) Yoder, Chouteau, Oklahoma

December 11, 2003
Pinecraft, Florida

Our fruit stand is pretty busy. Our strawberry farmer again has beautiful berries, and the watermelons and cantaloupes are still locally grown. Citrus seems to be a good crop.

Vera Overholt

Berry Lemonade Slush

½ cup lemonade drink mix

3 cups ice cubes

½ cup water

1 cup fresh or frozen strawberries

Blend all ingredients in a blender until slushy. Very refreshing! Makes 3 cups.

Regina Yoder, Summertown, Tennessee

November 19, 2003
Pinecraft, Florida

On Tuesday evening, Danny Miller had a motorcycle accident and was treated in the emergency room at Memorial Hospital. He had a broken kneecap. He was brought here for the night and the next day to be cared for until his surgery on Thursday morning. He's had a lot of pain, but seems to be coming along well. He attended part of the service yesterday. He is staying in Sam and Martha Hostetler's home at the present time. Becki Miller is his faithful nurse.

Bishop Lester and Sarah Gingerich left for Belize on Saturday. Lester and Edwin Weaver will officiate communion and minister in the various mission stations. We had our communion service on a Wednesday evening during the week of our revival meetings. Hughdelle Ysaguirre from Belize was our guest speaker.

Joe and Wilma Hostetler spruced up their ice cream shop across the street. They sell Big Olaf ice cream and sandwiches. Every Tuesday night there's a gospel sing on the premises.

The Thomas Peacheys own the Big Olaf Creamery at the corner of Beneva and Bahia Vista. They make the ice cream there and sell it in bulk.

Vera Overholt

Hum-De-Licious Mocha Shake

1 teaspoon instant coffee
   granules
¼ cup hot water
4 cups vanilla ice cream

¼ cup chocolate syrup
⅓ cup milk
1 tablespoon vanilla
1 teaspoon cinnamon (optional)

Dissolve instant coffee in hot water. Blend remaining ingredients together and serve as a refreshing cooler. Makes 1 blender pitcher full.

Rachel Marie Esh, Burkesville, Kentucky

Strawberry Mango Smoothie

1 cup fresh strawberries hulled
   and sliced
¼ cup orange juice

6 ice cubes (or more if desired)
½ cup mango, cubed

Place all ingredients into a blender and blend well. Makes 12 ounces.

Kathleen Schlabach, Sarasota, Florida

Citrus Orange Delight

⅓ cup frozen orange juice
   concentrate
¼ cup sugar
½ teaspoon vanilla

½ cup milk
5 or 6 ice cubes
½ cup water

Combine all ingredients in blender. Cover and blend until smooth. Serve immediately. Makes 3 servings.

Mrs. Mervin (Fannie Kay) Yoder, Chouteau, Oklahoma

Energy Drink

2 tablespoons apple cider vinegar
1 cup grape juice
1 cup apple juice

1 cup pineapple juice
1 cup cranberry juice

Mix well. Drink one or two cupfuls daily.

Kate Graber, Arthur, Illinois

June 13, 2007
Sunnyside Amish Mennonite Church, Sarasota, Florida

Overcast skies and little rain lead to sunburns, something we're seeing a lot of here. Not everybody waits for the winter to do their vacationing in Florida. Pinecraft is still mostly empty, though there has been some activity at Overholt's Produce. The sound of hammers and saws has some folks wondering what's going on. The next couple of weeks should tell the story.

Conrad Beiler hosted the schoolboys' campout Friday night at Daniel Kropf's in Myakka City. Jumping off the twelve-foot-high diving board into the swimming pond was a highlight for them. Grilled rabbit and hot dogs were on the menu.

The Bishop Lester Gingeriches are planning to return from Belize on Tuesday, and Paul Yoder left for Greensburg, Kansas, last Monday for tornado cleanup. This is no small task, considering the entire town was wiped away, leaving only concrete roadways and debris in its aftermath.

Minister Bill Yoder had the opening in church and shared some current events in his message about nonresistance. It seems a U.S. senator and another fellow in legislature had an exchange of words. This led to one of them getting (purposely) poked in the eye by the other's fist.

Sherry Gore, Pinecraft, Florida

Mocha

3 teaspoons creamer
¾ teaspoon instant coffee
3 teaspoons sugar

sprinkle of cinnamon
¾ teaspoon cocoa

Mix and add to a cup of hot milk. A delicious drink for the children while the adults are having coffee.

Mrs. Manny (Fannie) Troyer, Cleveland, North Carolina

Cappuccino Mix

3 cups powdered milk
1¼ cups Nesquik
3 cups French vanilla creamer

¾ cup instant coffee, scant
1½ – 2 cups powdered sugar

Combine all ingredients. Add ¼ cup dry mix to 8 – 10 ounce mug of hot water — more if desired. Store in airtight container. Yield: 10 cups dry mix.

Mrs. Lester (Ruth) Gingerich, Burkesville, Kentucky

Party Mix

I remember well how excited the children at school were when it was Ruth's turn to bring snack. This party mix was everyone's favorite.

assorted cereals and pretzels
1 cup butter, melted
2 tablespoons Worcestershire
  sauce

1 tablespoon celery salt
3 teaspoons Lawry's seasoned salt
1 tablespoon onion salt

Use this recipe to season 5 boxes of cereal. Gather different kinds of cereal or snacks such as Corn and Rice Chex, Cheerios, Kix, Bugles, pretzels, or whatever else you desire. Mix cereals together. Combine all other ingredients and pour over cereal. Mix well. Bake in jelly roll pans 1 hour at 250°, stirring every 15 minutes. Store in airtight containers.

Mrs. Lester (Ruth) Gingerich, Burkesville, Kentucky

Spiced Pretzels

These pretzels have a surprise zip to them!

1 pound pretzel twists
½ teaspoon lemon pepper
½ cup vegetable oil
½ teaspoon dill weed

1 package original Hidden Valley
 Ranch dressing mix
¼ teaspoon garlic salt

Place pretzels in bowl. Mix remaining ingredients; stir until blended. Pour over pretzels and toss well. Place on cookie sheet and bake 40 minutes at 250°, stirring every 10 minutes. Increase or decrease seasoning according to taste.

Kathleen Schlabach, Sarasota, Florida

Amish Peanut Butter

Also called "Church Spread," this is a staple in many Amish homes.

2 cups brown sugar
1 pint marshmallow crème
1 cup water (bring to boil
 and cool)

¼ cup dark corn syrup
2 cups peanut butter

Whip together until thoroughly mixed. Makes 7½ cups. (See color plate 9 for illustration.)

Sarah M. Miller, Sarasota, Florida

November 18, 2009
Sunnyside Amish Mennonite Church, Sarasota, Florida

The ladies had a delightful time oohing and aahing over the baby as we gathered together over sparkling punch, meats, cheese with crackers, and baked goodies at a shower held for Mrs. David (Wanda) Yoder Friday evening at her house. Baby Preston attended church yesterday for the first time.

Sherry Gore, Pinecraft, Florida

Pimento Cheese Spread

½ pound processed cheese,
shredded

¼ cup finely chopped pimentos
½ cup mayonnaise

In a large bowl combine cheese with mayonnaise and pimentos until well blended. Keep refrigerated. Makes 3 cups spread for sandwiches.

Anna Wengerd, Sarasota, Florida

Pennsylvania Punch

4 cups milk
2 quarts orange sherbet

1 quart vanilla ice cream
1 (2-liter) bottle lemon-lime soda

Beat together milk, sherbet, and ice cream in a pretty punch bowl. Pour soda over top and serve.

Shannon Torkelson, Alberta, Canada

3. Root Beer Float, *Made with Quick Homemade Root Beer, recipe page 55*

4. Gingerbread Waffles, *recipe page 43*

5. Orange Marmalade, *recipe page 233*

6. Honey Wheat Bread and Lisa's Homemade White Bread, *recipes pages 21 and 22*

7. Amish Church Dinner, *recipe page 113*

8. Dippy Eggs and Corn Mush with Tomato Gravy, *recipes pages 41 and 47*

9. Amish Peanut Butter and Strawberry Jelly, *recipes pages 62 and 232*

11. Seafood Chowder, *recipe page 146*

12. Cranberry Salad, Turkey Stuffing ("Filling Balls"), and Dutch Dinner Rolls, *recipes pages 77, 111, and 30*

13. Amish Bean Soup, *recipe page 75*

14. Hand-Breaded Pork Chops and Creamy Country Gravy, with Red-Skin Mashed Potatoes, *recipes pages 117 and 100*

15. Turkey (or Chicken) Biscuit Skillet, *recipe page 110*

Soups and Salads

Chili Soup

1 pound ground beef
1 small onion, chopped
1 teaspoon salt
¼ teaspoon pepper
1 pint chili or kidney beans (1
    15-ounce can)

1 teaspoon chili powder
¼ cup brown sugar
1 teaspoon Worcestershire sauce
1 pint chili sauce
1 – 1½ quarts tomato juice

Brown ground beef and onion; season with salt and pepper. Meanwhile in a 4-quart Dutch oven, heat over low heat beans, chili powder, brown sugar, Worcestershire sauce, chili sauce, and tomato juice. Add ground beef mixture in sauce. Simmer 1 – 2 hours.

Mrs. Earl (Fannie) Miller, Sarasota, Florida

Corn Chowder

4 slices bacon
1 tablespoon celery, minced
1 tablespoon green pepper,
   minced
1 tablespoon onion, minced
2 cups corn

2 potatoes, cooked
1 cup water
4 cups milk
parsley, chopped
salt and pepper to taste

Cut bacon in small pieces; place in pan. Add celery, green pepper, and onion. Fry together until bacon is brown. Add corn and sauté 3 minutes. Add chopped potatoes and 1 cup water. Cover and cook slowly 30 minutes. Add milk and heat to boiling. Add chopped parsley and seasoning. Makes 4 servings.

Sarah Joy Beiler, Pinecraft, Florida

Cheesy Turkey or Chicken Chowder

¼ cup butter
1 medium onion, diced
1 quart broth, add water if needed
1 tablespoon salt
1 cup potatoes, diced
1 cup carrots, diced

1 cup celery, diced
2 cups milk
⅓ cup flour
2 cups cooked turkey or chicken,
   diced
1 cup Velveeta cheese

Melt butter in 4- to 5-quart saucepan. Add chopped onion and sauté until tender; add broth, water, and salt. Bring to a boil. Add potatoes, carrots, and celery. Cook until soft, then add milk and flour. Bring to a boil again, stirring constantly. Add meat and remove from heat. Then add cheese and let it melt. Variation: Ham cubes can be used instead of chicken, seasoned with ham base. Makes 7 – 8 servings.

Mrs. John (Sadie) Esh, Burkesville, Kentucky

Rivel Soup

2 quarts whole milk

2 cups flour

2 eggs

1 teaspoon salt

½ teaspoon pepper or less

2 tablespoons butter, browned

Heat milk. Mix flour, eggs, salt, and pepper together to make crumbly lumps. Put into hot milk. Bring to boil. Simmer until "rivels" are done, 20 minutes. Try to have lumps not too big and stir to keep from scorching. Fold in the butter. Season with more salt as needed. Makes 10 – 12 ½-cup servings.

Mary Ellen Miller, Pleasantville, Tennessee

Cheeseburger Soup

1 pound ground beef

¼ cup chopped onion

1½ cups water

3 teaspoons beef bouillon

½ teaspoon salt

2 cups cubed red potatoes

1 celery rib, thinly sliced

3 tablespoons flour

2½ cups milk, divided

1 cup (4 ounces) shredded
  cheddar cheese

Ready in 1 hour or less. In a large saucepan, cook beef and onion over medium heat until meat is no longer pink; drain well. Stir in the water, bouillon, and salt. Add potatoes and celery. Bring to a boil; reduce heat. Cover and simmer 15 – 20 minutes or until potatoes are tender. Combine flour and ½ cup milk until smooth; gradually stir into beef mixture. Bring to a boil; cook and stir 2 minutes or until thickened and bubbly. Stir in 2 cups milk and shredded cheese until melted. Makes 7 servings.

Mrs. Paul E. (Mary) Miller, Pinecraft, Florida

Use a heavy stockpot when making cream soups to prevent scorching.

Potato Soup

1 can cream of chicken soup
16 ounces heavy whipping cream
32 ounce carton chicken broth
10 – 15 potatoes (cut in small
  pieces)

1 (8 ounce) container sour cream
12 slices bacon, fried crisp
  and broken into pieces,
  or 1 (3 ounce) of bacon bits
seasoned salt

Heat soup, cream, and chicken broth on medium heat. Add potatoes to this mixture and cook until done (keep on medium heat). When potatoes are tender, turn heat to low, and add sour cream, bacon, and seasoned salt to taste. Makes 15 servings.

Ida Yoder Hall, Greenville, Tennessee

Vegetable Soup

1 large soup bone or ribs of beef
½ stalk celery
2 cups diced potatoes
½ can whole corn or 4 ears
  of corn
2 large onions
1 cup shredded cabbage

½ pint string beans, cut fine
1 can tomatoes or 4 ripe tomatoes
1 cup lima beans
3 large carrots
parsley leaves
⅛ cup rice (optional)
¼ cup barley (optional)

In a stockpot with enough water to cover, cook soup bone or meat until done. Add vegetables and parsley. Cook ½ hour or until vegetables are tender. If rice and barley are used, cook separate or put in kettle with meat.

Rebecca Fisher, Pinecraft, Florida

Spread love everywhere you go;
first of all in your own home!
Mrs. John (Sadie) Esh

Cheesy Bean Soup

½ cup chopped onion

1 pound ham, chopped or cubed

3 tablespoons butter

2 cans great Northern beans

3 cups milk

1 teaspoon salt

½ teaspoon pepper

5 slices white American cheese

Fry onion and ham in butter. Add the beans and heat well. Add the rest of ingredients and heat hot enough to serve. Quick and easy. Makes 4 servings.

Mary Zook, Pennsylvania

Cream of Broccoli Soup

6 slices bacon

½ cup chopped onion

6 cups raw potatoes, shredded

1 teaspoon chicken soup base

1 can chicken broth

1 head broccoli

3 cups boiling water

3 tablespoons butter

4 tablespoons flour

2 quarts milk

2 teaspoons salt

½ pound Velveeta cheese

Fry bacon until crisp, then crumble. Sauté onion in bacon grease. Transfer to 8-quart saucepan, and add potatoes, chicken soup base, chicken broth, finely chopped broccoli, and boiling water. Cook until potatoes are well done. Melt butter, add flour, and blend; add milk and salt. Mix together and add Velveeta cheese in cubes until blended (do not boil after adding cheese). Serve with crackers. Makes 12 – 14 1-cup servings.

Sarah Zehr, Goshen, Indiana

Tomato Soup

Tomato soup — a grilled cheese sandwich's best friend!

4 cups chopped fresh tomatoes	2 tablespoons flour
¼ small onion, diced	1 teaspoon salt
4 whole cloves	¼ teaspoon black pepper
2 cups chicken broth or water	2 teaspoons sugar, scant
2 tablespoons butter	

In a stockpot over medium heat, combine tomatoes, onion, cloves, and chicken broth. Let boil for about 20 minutes. Remove from heat and put through a strainer. Melt butter in same stockpot over medium heat. Stir in flour and cook until medium brown. Gradually whisk in a bit of the tomato mixture so that no lumps form, then stir in the rest. Season with salt, pepper, and sugar to taste. Makes 6 cups.

Sherry Gore, Pinecraft, Florida

October 31, 2009

Sunnyside Amish Mennonite Church, Sarasota, Florida

Snowbirds planning a trip down south this winter should be delighted to find the Pinecraft Park is sporting not only a brand-new basketball court, but a new boat ramp as well.

Daughter Shannon (eighteen) has moved in temporarily with Amish Henry and Sarah while her room is being worked on. While I was at her place Friday, she took me by surprise when she asked, "Would you like to come to a cocktail party tonight? I'm having one." I'm certain my eyebrows furrowed as I said, "Shannon, do you know what a cocktail party is?" "Sure, look what I bought," she said. With all seriousness, she reached into her little fridge, turned around, held up a package, and exclaimed, "Cocktail shrimp!"

Sherry Gore, Pinecraft, Florida

Taco Soup

1 pound ground beef

1 small onion

1½ quarts tomato juice

1 teaspoon sugar

1 (15 ounce) can corn

1 (15 ounce) can chili beans

1 package taco seasoning

corn chips, crushed

shredded cheddar cheese

⅓ cup sour cream

Fry ground beef and onion. Add tomato juice, sugar, corn, beans, and taco seasoning. Cook all together. Serve over crushed chips and sprinkle cheese on top. Add a heaping spoonful of sour cream on top.

Mrs. Andrew (Ruth) Overholt, Pinecraft, Florida

May 7, 2008
Sunnyside Amish Mennonite Church, Sarasota, Florida

We had a full house this weekend, with company from South America, Missouri, Kentucky, and North Carolina. I was expecting Mrs. Joe (Sarah) Beiler, seventeen-year-old Judith, and ten-year-old Nelson, residents of Ixiamas, Bolivia, to bring supper in at 6:30 p.m. Coming along were several girls from down south. They offered to come and sing and pray with Jacinda. When the phone rang at 6:00 p.m., I was surprised to hear Amos Schwartz's voice (Salem, Missouri) on the other end. He and wife, Rhoda's, parents, the Harry Troyers of Burkesville, Kentucky, were only thirty miles outside Sarasota, heading our way. "Sherry," he said, "can we sleep in your barn?"

These were old friends from our Burkesville days. I ran to Troyer's Dutch Heritage Bakery to fetch some rolls and Amish peanut butter, and to maybe find a big stone on the way to stretch the pot of soup.

What fun to come home to a houseful of friends — some old and some new. Everyone either knew the other, had heard of them, or were related in some way. It reminded me of what we might experience in heaven one day. Helen Mast, formerly of Bolivia, presently living in North Carolina, joined us, along with her three girls, as did Linda Andriaccio, a Sarasota local. Sarah was embarrassed, she said, to be bringing such a large kettle of chicken potpie stew, but I told her, "This is great; now we don't need to add the stone!"

Sherry Gore, Pinecraft, Florida

Chicken Potpie (Stew)

1 (4-pound) chicken cut into serving size pieces	1 teaspoon salt
	4 medium-size potatoes, sliced
water to cover	2 tablespoons minced parsley

Potpie Dough

2 cups flour	½ teaspoon salt
2 eggs	2 – 3 tablespoons water

Cook chicken and debone. Season with salt. Return meat to broth, add potatoes and potpie dough squares, simmering 20 minutes. Add parsley and serve.

To make potpie dough, make a well in the flour and add eggs and salt. Work together to make a stiff dough. If too dry, add a bit of water. Roll out dough as thin as possible and cut into one-inch squares with a knife or pastry wheel.

Vera Kipfer, Pinecraft, Florida

I once had a pet hen named Henrietta who took to sitting on my shoulder while I was cooking. I used to think it was her fondness for me but now realize she was simply trying to stay alive.
Sherry Gore

May 28, 2008
Sunnyside Amish Mennonite Church, Sarasota, Florida

Nathan Overholt and Wilmer Miller brought the boys back from their hunting trip to Kentucky in one piece. They proclaimed it both a fun and profitable trip, and like most boys their ages, they returned with a lot of wildlife tales to tell. The snakes they caught were about five feet long, and the ones that got away, well, you can just imagine how big they were. They did get plenty of work done on the house they plan to stay in for the men's hunting trip this fall. Twelve-year-old Tyler was so grimy upon his return that you could see ground-in dirt on him after his second shower, so back he went for a third try.

Sherry Gore, Pinecraft, Florida

November 19, 2009
Sunnyside Amish Mennonite Church, Sarasota, Florida

Recently Nathan Overholt found a wandering calf out by Daniel Kropf's place in Myakka City. The owner told Nathan he could keep it if he bottle-fed it. Not wanting to leave it behind while on their hunting trip last week in Kentucky, he and Janet made a bed for the calf on their trailer. While driving on the interstate, first the hay, then the plywood blew out; then the calf did too. Nathan stopped his SUV and struggled to get the calf off the median before it ran out in traffic, fearing it would get hit by a semi truck. Finally, he caught the calf and put it in the Suburban. Janet sat on it and gave it a bottle.

Sherry Gore, Pinecraft, Florida

Wild Rice and Beef Soup

1 pound lean ground beef, crumbled
½ cup butter or margarine
¼ cup finely chopped onion
¾ cup flour
6 cups ready-to-serve chicken broth

4 cups cooked wild rice
1 cup shredded carrots
1 – 2 teaspoons seasoned salt
1 teaspoon pepper
¾ – 1 cup milk

In a 6-quart Dutch oven or stockpot, cook meat over medium heat until it is no longer pink. Drain. Remove meat and set aside. Wipe out pot. In same pot, melt butter over medium heat. Add onion. Cook until tender. Stir in flour. Cook 1 minute, stirring constantly. Gradually whisk in broth. Cook 6 – 8 minutes or until soup comes to a boil, stirring constantly. Cook 1 minute, stirring constantly. Stir in beef, rice, carrots, salt, and pepper. Simmer 5 minutes, stirring occasionally. Stir in milk. Cook 4 – 6 minutes, or until heated through, stirring occasionally. (Do not boil.) Garnish soup with snipped fresh parsley or chives.

Mrs. Daniel (Lena) Kropf, Myakka City, Florida

With the onset of another "season," and the recession lingering, Pinecraft business persons as a whole remain upbeat. If money is tight up north, the tourists will still come, for they have sand in their shoes. Not for nothing is Pinecraft called "the most unique village in the world." Todd Emerich, general manager of Yoder's Restaurant, said with cheery confidence, "I think we're going to have a great season. Tourism is going to be good."

Sales at Yoder's are up sharply as a result of the restaurant having been featured in the nationally syndicated TV show *Man v. Food*. When I inquired of Mr. Emerich what it is that he tries to provide to the public, his answer came promptly: "Value and quality."

Daniel Fisher, editor, *Pinecraft Pauper*

Amish Bean Soup

This soup is served for the noon meal at some churches on Communion Sunday.

½ pound dried white beans
1 onion, chopped
1 teaspoon vegetable oil
5 cups water
one ham hock
½ cup mashed potatoes (optional)

½ teaspoon salt
¼ teaspoon dried thyme
½ teaspoon black pepper
½ pound bacon, cut into small pieces

Place beans in a Dutch oven; add water to cover. Bring to a boil; boil 2 minutes and reduce heat. Simmer on low until beans are softened. Drain and rinse beans, discarding liquid. Sauté onions in oil 2 minutes. Stir in the beans, water, ham, potatoes, salt, thyme, and pepper. Add bacon pieces. Bring to a boil. Reduce heat; cover and simmer 1½ hours. Makes 7 servings. (See color plate 13 for illustration.)

Sherry Gore, Pinecraft, Florida

Chicken Corn Noodle Soup

1 whole chicken
1 teaspoon salt
2 carrots
2 onions

2 celery ribs
12 ounces corn
½ pound homemade egg noodles
½ teaspoon black pepper

Place chicken in large kettle. Add salt and enough water to completely cover chicken. Simmer 1½ hours. Slice vegetables. When chicken easily falls off bone, remove from pot; let cool. Add sliced vegetables and corn to broth and continue to simmer. Debone chicken and return meat to kettle along with noodles. Bring to a boil and simmer on low to medium heat 10 minutes. Add pepper. More salt may be added for flavor.

Sherry Gore, Pinecraft, Florida

THINK THICK

- Dry instant mashed potato flakes make a good thickener for recipes like barbecue beef and soups. They're also useful when making potato pancakes and salmon patties.

TIP

- To thicken recipes such as chili, soup, stews, and spaghetti sauce without changing the color, use Clear Jel, PermaFlo, or ThermaFlo. These thickeners work best when used with acidic foods. Use ¼ cup per 1 quart liquid. Bring liquid to a boil before adding thickener.

- Sure-Jell is a natural fruit pectin used in making jams and jellies that allows you to use approximately one-quarter less sugar than you normally would and still produce a jam that sets up nicely.

- Cornstarch is a super thickener that works great in gravies and puddings. When blended with flour, cornstarch makes a better texture for cakes and pies.

Homemade Cream Soup

½ cup butter
6 tablespoons flour
2 cups milk

2 cubes (or 2 teaspoons) chicken bouillon
salt and black pepper to taste

Melt butter in a saucepan. Add flour and make a paste. Add milk and bouillon cubes. Cook over low heat until thickened. Add salt and pepper to taste. Add more milk when adding the other soup ingredients, depending on the thickness you desire. Recipe equals one can prepared condensed soup.

Sherry Gore, Pinecraft, Florida

Variations

Add 1 cup of any of the following to your soup base:

steamed broccoli

sautéed mushrooms

boiled potato chunks

shredded or chopped chicken

sautéed chopped celery

shredded cheese or Velveeta

Kalte Suppe (Cold Soup)

2 cups fresh fruit in season

4 slices homemade bread

2 cups cold milk

Place fruit slices in soup bowl. Break bread into bite-size pieces and add to fruit. Pour milk over top. This makes an especially good dish in warm weather. Makes two servings.

Sherry Gore, Pinecraft, Florida

Cranberry Salad

1 (3 ounce) package raspberry or cherry Jell-O

1 cup hot water

1 package unflavored gelatin

1 tablespoon lemon juice

1 (20 ounce) can crushed pineapple

1 can whole-berry cranberry sauce

1 cup diced celery

½ cup chopped pecans

zest of 1 orange

Combine Jell-O and hot water. Stir until Jell-O is dissolved. Combine unflavored gelatin and lemon juice; add to Jell-O mixture. Add remaining ingredients to Jell-O mixture and stir. Pour into a mold or 9x9-inch pan. Makes 9 servings. (See color plate 12 for illustration.)

Mrs. Paul E. (Mary) Miller, Pinecraft, Florida

Carrot and Egg Salad

½ cup water
1 package unflavored gelatin
1 teaspoon salt
½ cup sugar
juice of ½ lemon

½ cup mayonnaise
4 hard-boiled eggs
2 cups grated carrots
2 cups celery, cut

To ½ cup water add 1 package gelatin in saucepan. Stir over low heat until hot. Do not boil. Combine gelatin with remaining ingredients and pour into 2 medium-size molds. Let set. Refrigerate. Makes 8 servings.

Lavina Kauffman, Pinecraft, Florida

Celery Seed Dressing

⅔ cup sugar
1 teaspoon dry mustard
1 teaspoon salt
¼ onion, grated

⅓ cup vinegar
¾ cup salad oil
1 tablespoon celery seed

Mix sugar, mustard, and salt. Add grated onion. Add alternatively the vinegar and salad oil, and beat. Add the celery seed last. Makes about 1½ cups.

Laura Yoder, Sarasota, Florida

Poppy Seed Dressing

½ cup cider vinegar
1 teaspoon ground mustard
½ cup sugar
½ teaspoon salt

1 garlic clove
1 cup vegetable oil
1 green onion
4 teaspoons poppy seeds

Blend ingredients in blender until well mixed.

Sherry Gore, Pinecraft, Florida

Pinecraft Winter Salad

4 cups mixed salad greens

1 cup Mandarin orange slices, fresh in season tangerines, oranges, or seedless clementines

1 cup fresh strawberries

½ cup dried cranberries

½ cup toasted nuts of your choice — pecans, almonds, or macadamia nuts

1 cup blue cheese crumbles

Toss all ingredients together and serve with your favorite salad dressing. Makes 4 servings. (See color plate 19 for illustration.)

Sherry Gore, Pinecraft, Florida

January 20, 2010
Sunnyside Amish Mennonite Church, Sarasota, Florida

The great freeze of Sarasota 2010 is history. The patchy brown lawns and dead tropical foliage are not something we are accustomed to seeing here.

The Thomas Peacheys of the Amish Church are known for their delicious Big Olaf ice cream, but Leah Peachey has found a way to make Sarasota even sweeter. Last Wednesday was the debut of the Philippi Farmers' Market, held every Wednesday, and Leah was featured in the *Sarasota Herald Tribune*, selling her fresh, homemade doughnuts at the market.

Spinach Salad

4 cups cut-up spinach

1 cup minced parsley

1 cup mushrooms

2 medium tomatoes

2 celery ribs

1 can bean sprouts, drained

1 cup sunflower seeds

1½ cups shredded cheese

¼ teaspoon salt

¼ teaspoon pepper

garlic salt

Dressing

½ cup vegetable oil	3 tablespoons chili sauce
¼ teaspoon pepper	¼ cup vinegar
¼ cup chopped onion	1½ teaspoons Worcestershire
¼ cup honey	sauce

In large salad bowl combine spinach, parsley, mushrooms (slightly sautéed), tomatoes, celery, bean sprouts, sunflower seeds, cheese, and seasonings. Combine dressing ingredients in a jar with a lid and shake well. The dressing can be served with tossed salad or fruit salad also. Makes 4 servings.

Sovilla Mast, Pinecraft, Florida

Marinated Vegetable Salad

1 can green beans, drained	1 jar sliced red pimento, drained
1 cup sliced green onions	4 stalks celery, diced
1 can baby peas, drained	1 can sliced water chestnuts,
½ cup diced bell pepper	drained
1 can shoepeg corn, drained	

Dressing

1 cup sugar	¾ cup canola oil
½ cup vinegar	1 teaspoon salt

Mix dressing ingredients and boil to dissolve sugar. Pour over vegetables. Best if made a day or two ahead so vegetables can marinate. When ready to serve, drain sauce or use slotted spoon.

Esther Schlabach, Sarasota, Florida

Florida Salad

8 ounces miniature
  marshmallows
6 firm bananas, sliced

1 (20 ounce) can pineapple
  tidbits, drained (reserve juice)
½ cup chopped nuts

Mix marshmallows, bananas, pineapple, and nuts together. Chill.

Sherry Gore, Pinecraft, Florida

Dressing

2 tablespoons flour
1 cup sugar
2 eggs, well beaten

1 cup cream, whipped, or 8
  ounces nondairy whipped
  topping

Mix flour and sugar; stir into reserved pineapple juice and add eggs. Cook over low heat or in double boiler until thick. Cool. When cold, fold in cream or nondairy whipped topping and add to fruit. Oranges may be added if desired. Makes 10 servings.

Mrs. John Henry (Minnie) Schmucker, Burkesville, Kentucky

Pineapple Cheese Salad

1 (20 ounce) can crushed
  pineapple, undrained
1 cup water
1 cup sugar
1 tablespoon cornstarch, heaping

2 tablespoons flour
1 egg
1 cup Spanish peanuts
1 cup Colby jack cheese

In saucepan bring pineapple and water to boil. Combine sugar, cornstarch, flour, and egg. Add small portion of hot mixture to egg mixture; mix until smooth, then slowly pour into hot mixture. Stir until smooth and thickened. Cool. Just before serving, add peanuts and cubed cheese. Makes 8 servings.

Mrs. Elmer (Millie) Beachy, Sarasota, Florida

Macaroni Salad

1 pound macaroni
½ cup pickle relish
¾ cup sugar
¼ cup vinegar
¾ cup chopped celery
1 tablespoon celery seed
2 cups salad dressing
　(Miracle Whip)

1 tablespoon parsley
1 cup mayonnaise
1 teaspoon mustard
12 hard-boiled eggs
½ teaspoon turmeric
¼ cup chopped carrots
1 (5 ounce) can evaporated milk
　(optional)

Cook macaroni in boiling water with 1 teaspoon salt 10 minutes. Rinse in colander. Combine remaining ingredients and add macaroni. Makes 15 servings.

Hannah Stoltzfus, East Waterford, Pennsylvania

Overnight Potato Salad

12 cups shredded potatoes
12 hard-boiled eggs
3 tablespoons mustard
4 teaspoons salt
1½ cups chopped onions
2 cups sugar

1½ cups chopped celery
½ cup milk
1 cup sour cream
3 cups Miracle Whip or 3 cups
　mayonnaise and 3 tablespoons
　vinegar

Cook and shred potatoes and eggs. Place in large bowl. Mix remaining ingredients and pour over salad. Refrigerate overnight. Makes 20 servings.

Malinda Miller, Indiana

Grape Salad

4 pounds seedless grapes (washed and drained)
1 (8 ounce) package cream cheese
8 ounces sour cream
1½ cups powdered sugar
1 teaspoon lemon juice
8 ounces whipped topping
4 tablespoons chopped pecans
2 tablespoons brown sugar

Cut grapes in half. Soften cream cheese and mix with sour cream and sugar. Add lemon juice and stir. Fold grapes into creamed mixture. Top with whipped cream. Sprinkle with pecans and brown sugar. Mix and refrigerate until serving. Makes 8 servings.

Mrs. Levi M. Schrock, Arthur, Illinois

Crunchy Salad

⅔ cup salad oil
½ cup wine vinegar
3 tablespoons soy sauce
½ teaspoon salt
½ teaspoon garlic powder
½ teaspoon pepper
1 cup sugar
1 head iceberg lettuce
1 head romaine lettuce
1 head broccoli
3 green onions
4 tablespoons butter
1 cup slivered almonds
1 package Ramen noodles

Combine first seven ingredients (through sugar) in blender. Blend until well mixed. Tear lettuce, cut up broccoli and onions, and mix together. In a skillet melt butter, and place almonds and noodles in butter. Fry together until brown. Just before serving, mix all together. Note: We really like the crunchy topping, so I usually double the butter, almonds, and noodles. Unused salad gets soggy. (Do not substitute cider vinegar for wine vinegar.) Makes 15 servings.

Amanda Yoder, founder of Yoder's Restaurant, Pinecraft, Florida

Cabbage Slaw

1 large head cabbage

2 large onions

1 green pepper

1 cup sugar

1 tablespoon salt

1 cup vinegar

1 teaspoon celery seed

1 teaspoon dry mustard

2 tablespoons sugar

¾ cup vegetable oil

Chop up vegetables. Mix in 1 cup sugar. Combine all other ingredients in saucepan, bring to a boil, pour over vegetables, and marinate overnight in refrigerator. Makes 10 – 12 cups.

Emma Hochstetler, Millersburg, Ohio

Triple Orange Salad

2½ cups water

1 box orange Jell-O

1 box instant vanilla pudding

1 box tapioca pudding

1 can mandarin oranges, drained

2 cups whipped topping

Bring water to a full boil. Add Jell-O and puddings. Boil again. Take from heat and cool. Add mandarin oranges. Add whipped topping. Makes 8 ½-cup servings.

Shannon Torkelson, Alberta, Canada

- *In 1937 a bushel of oranges sold for 50¢ in Sarasota.*
- *Grapefruits were 25¢ a bushel.*
- *In 2012 oranges sold for $24.95 a bushel.*
- *Grapefruits fetched $22.95.*

Cauliflower Pea Salad

5 cups cut up cauliflower
1 cup diced celery
2 cups frozen peas
½ cup chopped onion
½ cup plain yogurt or sour cream

⅓ cup Miracle Whip
1½ teaspoons dill weed
1 teaspoon salt-free herb blend
salt to taste
sugar, if desired

Combine first four ingredients (through onion). Combine yogurt and rest of ingredients. Mix well. Add to cauliflower mixture. Toss to coat. Keep in refrigerator until ready to serve. Makes 16 servings.

Edith Good, Wooster, Ohio

Special Occasion Salad

2 cups diced or cubed pineapple, well drained
½ pound seeded grapes cut in half

10 large marshmallows, cut in 3 pieces (I use small ones accordingly)
½ cup chopped nuts

Dressing

1 cup brown sugar
2 tablespoons lemon juice
pinch of salt
2 tablespoons butter

2 eggs, well beaten
8 ounces whipped topping
1 teaspoon vanilla

Mix together fruit, marshmallow, and nuts. In a saucepan, combine brown sugar, lemon juice, butter, and salt. When butter is melted, stir in beaten eggs, stirring constantly about 10 minutes or until well cooked. Cool. Add whipped topping and vanilla, and mix with the fruit, marshmallow, and nuts. This can be made ahead. I use red grapes, and you can use more whipped topping if desired. Makes 6 cups.

Irene Schlabach, Sarasota, Florida

Apple Salad

6 apples, peeled and chopped
1 – 2 stalks celery, diced

½ cup walnuts, chopped

Dressing

1 cup water
¾ cup sugar
1 teaspoon vinegar
¼ teaspoon salt

1 – 2 tablespoons cornstarch
¼ cup cream
1 teaspoon vanilla

Bring the first 4 dressing ingredients to a boil. Add a little water to the cornstarch and pour into the boiling mixture to thicken, stirring constantly. Add the cream and vanilla. (Add more cream if 2 tablespoons cornstarch are used.) Mix in apples, walnuts, and celery. Makes 6 – 8 servings.

Vera Overholt, Pinecraft, Florida

Tomato Salad

3 tomatoes, diced
1 stalk celery, cut up

2 hard-boiled eggs, diced

Dressing

1 tablespoon vinegar
½ teaspoon salt
2 tablespoons sugar

2 tablespoons mayonnaise
    or Miracle Whip

Mix tomatoes, celery, and eggs. Stir together the dressing ingredients and mix into salad. Makes 6 servings.

Esther (Burkholder) Sauder, Danville, Pennsylvania

October 29, 2008
Sunnyside Amish Mennonite Church, Sarasota, Florida

My one small connection to politics got its roots in Pinecraft. Some years back I posted a sign on the Amish post office bulletin board. It read, "Mennonite Woman Will Take In Ironing." That afternoon I got a call from Florida Republican State Senator Lisa Carlton. I started working for her that day, and a wonderful friendship ensued. Later, when we were living in Burkesville, Kentucky, we would meet at Yoder's Restaurant while down visiting. With seven children between us, the hostess would seat us at the round table in the center of the dining room, much to the chagrin of other customers.

Sherry Gore, Pinecraft, Florida

Ginger Ale Salad

2 packages unflavored gelatin
¼ cup water
1 cup boiling water
¾ cup sugar
juice of 1 lemon

2 cups ginger ale
1 cup sliced peaches, drained
1 cup pineapple chunks, drained
1 cup grapes, halved

Dressing

1 tablespoon flour
½ cup sugar
2 eggs, beaten

1½ tablespoons butter, melted
pineapple juice from medium size
can

Dissolve gelatin in ¼ cup water. Add boiling water to sugar. Add juice of lemon and ginger ale. Let jell; add fruit when thick and syrupy. Dressing: Mix flour with sugar. Add beaten eggs. Add melted butter and juice from medium size can of pineapple. Cook in double boiler until thick. Spread over Jell-O when ready to serve.

Vera Kipfer, Pinecraft, Florida

Tropical Chicken Salad

2 cups cooked chicken, cubed
1 cup chopped celery
1 cup mayonnaise
½ to 1 teaspoon curry powder
1 (20 ounce) can chunk
    pineapple, drained
2 large, firm bananas, sliced

1 (11 ounce) can mandarin
    oranges, drained
½ cup flaked coconut
salad greens (optional)
¾ cup salted peanuts or cashew
    halves

Place chicken and celery in a large bowl. Combine mayonnaise and curry powder. Add to chicken mixture and mix well. Cover and chill for at least 30 minutes. Before serving, add pineapple, bananas, oranges, and coconut; toss gently. Serve on salad greens if desired. Sprinkle with nuts. Makes 4 – 6 servings.

Esther Martin, Martinsburg, Pennsylvania

Buttermilk Chive Dressing

¾ cup buttermilk
1 tablespoon minced garlic clove
½ cup mayonnaise
½ teaspoon salt

2 tablespoons chopped fresh
    chives
¼ teaspoon fresh ground pepper
1 tablespoon minced green onion

Whisk together all ingredients. Cover and chill until ready to use. Makes 1½ cups.

Sherry Gore, Pinecraft, Florida

Honey Orange Salad Dressing

1¾ cups plain yogurt
2 tablespoons freshly squeezed
    lemon juice
¼ cup honey

2 tablespoons frozen orange juice
    concentrate
¾ teaspoon freshly grated orange
    rind
¼ teaspoon freshly grated ginger

Combine all ingredients and serve over fresh green salad leaves or fruit chunks.

Sherry Gore, Pinecraft, Florida

French Dressing (Dutch Oven)

2 cups vegetable oil
¾ cup ketchup
¾ cup vinegar
2 teaspoons salt

2 cups sugar
1 tablespoon Worcestershire sauce

Combine with mixer 10 minutes or in blender 2 minutes.

Annie (Mast) Graber, former owner of
Dutch Oven Restaurant, Sarasota, Florida

Sweet and Sour Dressing

1 small onion
3 teaspoons mustard
1 cup sugar
⅓ cup vinegar
1 teaspoon salt

1 cup vegetable oil
½ teaspoon pepper
¾ cup salad dressing
(Miracle Whip)
1 teaspoon celery seed

Combine ingredients in blender. Store in refrigerator.

Mary Zook, Dundee, Ohio

Hot Bacon Dressing for Dandelion Greens

2 slices bacon, cut up
1 egg

3 tablespoons sugar
3 tablespoons vinegar

Fry bacon and leave in skillet. Beat the egg, sugar, and vinegar together in a bowl. Add to the bacon and cook, stirring until thick. Serve over fresh, raw dandelion greens.

Sherry Gore, Pinecraft, Florida

Sweet and Sour Dressing

2½ cups sugar
1 – 2 tablespoons chopped onion
¾ cup vinegar
1½ teaspoons celery seed
1½ cups salad oil

1 teaspoon black pepper
½ cup salad dressing
   (Miracle Whip)
1 teaspoon salt
¼ cup prepared mustard

Mix well, then put in blender until very well blended.

Barbara Miller, Goshen, Indiana

Creamy French Dressing

1 cup mayonnaise
¼ teaspoon salt
3 tablespoons vinegar
¼ teaspoon Worcestershire sauce
¼ teaspoon garlic powder

3 tablespoons vegetable oil
½ teaspoon prepared mustard
½ cup white sugar
3 tablespoons ketchup

Blend ingredients until smooth. Makes 2 cups dressing.

Mrs. Glen (Ada) Miller, Millersburg, Ohio, and Sarasota, Florida

January 9, 2008
Sunnyside Amish Mennonite Church, Sarasota, Florida

The windows are open here at our home to let in the fresh air, but just a few days ago, many folks were scurrying around to protect their tropical plants and citrus trees. We woke up on Wednesday to 30 degrees. It was the first time folks were bundled up this winter as they were riding bikes in Pinecraft. The bike rack on Bahia Vista Street and Tuttle Avenue, at the Siesta Key bus stop, was just as full as ever. Some folks must be braver than others to venture out to the beach on such a day.

We've all likely heard the term "raining cats and dogs," but here in Florida we actually have iguanas falling from the sky. The freezing temperatures immobilize the reptiles, causing them to drop from their perches high in the treetops. Later in the day, when the sun is shining, the critters seem to miraculously wake up and scurry on up the trees again.

Several men were out to Bob Rapp's place in Sebring to help protect the beautiful foliage he grows in his plant nursery. Bob shared his appreciation to the brothers at church for helping him to prepare for what could have been a lot worse situation as the temperatures were not as severe as anticipated.

The schoolchildren are excited to have a tether ball put up in the play yard, but from the looks of it, one can't tell if it's the parents or the students having more fun.

Sherry Gore, Pinecraft, Florida

Fruity Florida Coleslaw

1 head cabbage, shredded
2 Florida oranges (or canned mandarin oranges)
1 (16 ounce) can pineapple chunks, drained
2 apples, chopped
1 cup red grapes, halved
1 whole banana, sliced
½ cup chopped walnuts
¼ cup sweetened coconut flakes
½ cup mayonnaise
1 tablespoon lemon juice
¾ cup nondairy whipped topping
1 tablespoon sugar
dash salt

Place cabbage, fruits, coconut, and nuts in large bowl. In small bowl mix remaining ingredients. Pour over cabbage mixture and serve in your prettiest glass dish.

Shannon Torkelson, Alberta, Canada

November 5, 2008
Sunnyside Amish Mennonite Church, Sarasota, Florida

It's official: winter is here. There were two yard sales in Pinecraft yesterday to usher in the new season. Another telltale sign of winter in Sarasota is the annual gathering held at Daniel and Lena Kropf's spread in Myakka City. The Sunnyside Church and a few invited friends headed out east Saturday for food, fun, and fishing. It was the week of this gathering a few years ago that I wrote my first "Letter from Home" for *The Budget*.

Folks enjoyed taco soup, chicken and noodles, and smoked turkey for supper, and Dave and Regina Stutzman organized several games to challenge the athletes among us. Sarah Alimowski and Christopher (Stanley) Mullet were the winners of the warty pumpkin throw. Anna Yoder took top billing in the apple peeling contest, unraveling her apple in one 39-inch piece. Sack races, tug-of-war, corn shelling, and wheelbarrow races kept everyone laughing. Some sat by the bonfire eating the s'mores the boys were roasting, while others gathered up front, singing hymns.

Sherry Gore, Pinecraft, Florida

Vegetables and Side Dishes

Fried Zucchini Patties

5 cups grated zucchini
1 tablespoon salt
1 teaspoon oregano
2 eggs

1 teaspoon basil
1 cup flour
½ tablespoon grated Parmesan
cheese

Combine all ingredients except cheese. Form patties and fry in skillet. Sprinkle with cheese while still hot. Makes 10 – 12 patties.

Vera Overholt, Pinecraft, Florida

December 14, 2009
Sunnyside Amish Mennonite Church, Sarasota, Florida

With Dave Beachy working as the Pinecraft real estate specialist, there seems to be as many SOLD signs in the village as there are FOR SALE signs from other realty companies. Dave sold the house we were renting on Good/Gilbert Avenue in just seven weeks; remarkable for this economy.

Yesterday the owners of Yoder's Amish Village (restaurant, gift shop, and market) held a Christmas Sunday brunch for their employees and guests. Just up the road, at Der Dutchman Restaurant, David Yoder and brother Timothy were busy making homemade ice cream for the 270 folks who turned out for the cowboy-themed employee Christmas party.

Speaking of cowboys, several more Torkelsons will be flying in from Alberta, Canada, on Thursday, and plan to stick around until the 24th. Their ninety-three-year-old grandmother, Martha Gingerich, lives in Pinecraft.

Sherry Gore, Pinecraft, Florida

Harvest Crew Potatoes

9 medium potatoes
seasoned salt
garlic salt
pepper

½ cup butter, melted
¼ cup Parmesan cheese
 (optional)
paprika (optional)

Preheat oven to 400°. Peel potatoes and cut them into strips. Place in greased 13x9-inch casserole dish. Lightly sprinkle with seasonings. Pour butter on top. Cover tightly with foil. Bake 1 hour. Sprinkle with Parmesan cheese and paprika if desired.

Anna Musser, Manheim, Pennsylvania

Delicious Onion Pie

¼ cup melted butter

1 cup crushed soda crackers

3 large onions, chopped

2 tablespoons butter

2 eggs, slightly beaten

¼ teaspoon salt

¼ teaspoon pepper

¾ cup milk

½ cup grated cheese

paprika

Preheat oven to 350°. Mix butter and crackers. Press into pie pan. Sauté onions in 2 tablespoons butter until tender to sweeten them. Place in cracker crust. Mix eggs, salt, pepper, and milk. Pour over pie. Bake 20 minutes. Sprinkle with cheese and paprika. Bake 10 – 15 minutes longer until done. Makes 8 servings.

Mary Ellen Mullet, Nappanee, Indiana

Scalloped Corn Supreme

1 (15 ounce) can cream style corn

1 cup milk

1 egg, well beaten

¼ cup finely chopped onion

3 tablespoons chopped canned pimiento

¾ teaspoon salt

½ cup Ritz cracker crumbs, buttered

Preheat oven to 350°. Heat corn and milk in medium pan on stovetop. Gradually stir in egg. Add remaining ingredients except buttered Ritz cracker crumbs. Pour into 8-inch baking dish. Top with buttered crumbs. Bake 20 minutes. Makes 6 – 8 servings.

Mrs. John Henry (Minnie) Schmucker, Burkesville, Kentucky

Glazed Carrots

2 cups carrots, peeled and cut
   into rounds
2 cups water

4 tablespoons butter
2 tablespoons brown sugar
2 tablespoons onion powder

Add water to carrots and cook over medium heat for 20 minutes or until soft. In a separate saucepan, melt butter, stirring in sugar and onion powder. Pour glaze onto drained carrots. Heat and stir. Makes 4½ cup servings. (See color plate 10 for illustration.)

Mrs. Raymond (Katie) Fisher, Newburg, Pennsylvania

Cabbage Casserole

1 head cabbage, cut up
1 onion, chopped
6 tablespoons butter
1 can cream of mushroom soup

8 ounces American cheese, cubed
salt and pepper to taste
1 cup dry bread crumbs

Cook cabbage in boiling water until tender; drain thoroughly. Preheat oven to 350°. In a large pan, sauté onions in 2 tablespoons butter. Add soup to onions and mix well with cheese. Stir bread crumbs in pan with 4 tablespoons butter until lightly browned. Spread over cabbage in an ungreased 2-quart baking pan. Bake 20 – 30 minutes. Makes 6 – 8 servings.

Susan Stoltzfus, Bird-in-Hand, Pennsylvania

Cheesy Corn

1½ cups corn, cooked and
   drained
3 tablespoons milk
8 ounces cream cheese
2 tablespoons sugar

2 tablespoons butter
6 slices white American cheese,
   cut up
3 tablespoons water

Combine all ingredients in slow cooker and cook on low 4 hours. Makes 4 cups.

Anna Musser, Manheim, Pennsylvania

May 12, 2004
Pinecraft, Florida

Today was our sewing group. We completed a number of dresses for girls in Haiti. The group is smaller since most of the snowbirds have returned north.

We had special guests here in the past few weeks. Deborah Shofstahl from Petersburg, Ohio, was here with a friend, Sue Thomas, from near Youngstown. Deborah is Sue's traveling companion. Sue has been deaf since she was eighteen months old. In spite of her disability, she became a skating champion when a child and also became an accomplished pianist. She knows sounds for music through vibrations. She was an FBI surveillant for more than three years and reads lips very well.

Vera Overholt

Chuck Wagon Beans

1 pound ground beef
1 medium onion, diced
1 green pepper, diced
½ pound bacon, cut into small
  pieces
1 (15.5 ounce) can great northern
  beans
1 (15.5 ounce) can kidney beans
1 (15.5 ounce) can lima beans

1 (15.5 ounce) can baked beans
½ teaspoon mustard
½ cup brown sugar
1 teaspoon garlic powder
½ cup white sugar
2 tablespoons molasses
¼ cup ketchup
dash of Worcestershire sauce

Preheat oven to 350°. Brown ground beef. Add onion and green pepper, and brown with ground beef. Fry bacon and add bacon and bacon drippings with beans and the other ingredients. Bake covered 1 hour; uncover and bake 30 minutes longer.

Elizabeth Peachey, Loganton, Pennsylvania

Amish Potato Cakes

2 eggs, separated
1 cup mashed potatoes
½ cup flour

½ teaspoon baking powder
1 cup milk
2 tablespoons onion, minced

Add egg yolks to mashed potatoes and mix well. Add flour and baking powder alternately with milk until smooth. Fold in stiffly beaten egg whites and onion. Use a large spoon to drop batter onto hot greased skillet. Turn when bottom is browned. May be eaten with sour cream or applesauce.

Cheesy Scalloped Potatoes

1 tablespoon butter
2 tablespoons flour
½ teaspoon salt
½ teaspoon pepper
¾ cup milk
2 cups cubed Velveeta

4 baking potatoes, sliced
½ cup sliced onions
½ cup cheddar cheese
4 bacon strips, cooked and
    crumbled and sprinkled on top

Preheat oven to 350°. Melt butter in saucepan; add flour, salt, and pepper. Stir until well blended. Add milk and cook until thickened; lower heat. Add Velveeta cheese and stir until melted. Do not boil after cheese is added. Grease 1-quart casserole dish and layer potatoes, some sauce, then some onions. Repeat layers. Top with cheddar cheese and cover. Bake 1 hour or more until potatoes are soft. Sprinkle with bacon just before serving.

Amanda Yoder, founder of Yoder's Restaurant, Pinecraft, Florida

Healthy Crunchy Zucchini Sticks

3 medium zucchinis
½ cup wheat germ
½ cup finely chopped almonds

¼ cup grated Parmesan cheese
½ teaspoon salt
¼ cup butter, melted

Preheat oven to 350°. Cut each zucchini lengthwise into fourths, then cut each quarter in half to form sticks. Mix wheat germ, almonds, cheese, and salt in plastic bag. Roll about 8 zucchini sticks at a time in butter until evenly coated. Lift with fork. Shake sticks in wheat germ mixture. Lay on ungreased cookie sheet. Bake about 15 minutes until crisp and tender. Makes 6 servings.

Mrs. Sam (Katie) Yoder, Rose Hill, Virginia

Brussels Sprouts in Onion Cream

1½ pounds Brussels sprouts	½ cup chopped onion
2 tablespoons butter	1 pint sour cream

Cook Brussels sprouts until tender. Sauté onions in butter until brown. Stir in sour cream and heat, stirring constantly. Add Brussels sprouts and mix well. Makes 10 servings.

Anna Beiler, Leola, Pennsylvania

Raber's Baked Beans

½ pound bacon, cut up	1 (15 ounce) can lima beans, drained
2 onions, cut fine	
1 large can pork and beans	1 cup brown sugar
1 (15 ounce) can kidney beans, drained	1 cup ketchup
	1 tablespoon mustard

Preheat oven to 350°. Cut up bacon and fry with onions. Mix all ingredients together and bake 1 hour. I add a little Worcestershire sauce. Makes 10 – 12 servings.

Mrs. Mary Raber, Millersburg, Ohio

Slow Cooker Potatoes

4 large potatoes, scrubbed
½ onion
½ teaspoon pepper
1 teaspoon salt

1 – 2 tablespoons butter
⅔ cup milk
slices of cheese (optional)

Slice potatoes and onion. Layer in slow cooker with seasonings, butter, and milk. Cook on high 3 – 4 hours. Add sliced cheese just before serving if desired. For a one-pot meal, add 1 cup diced ham or sausage, precooked and sliced. Serves 4 – 6 people. A wonderful dish to have waiting after church.

Sara Ann Petersheim, Narvon, Pennsylvania

Red-Skin Mashed Potatoes

8 medium-large size red potatoes
1 stick butter
1 clove garlic, minced

1 – 2 cups milk — depending
on size of potatoes
salt and pepper to taste

Boil potatoes with skin on until soft. Melt butter in a saucepan with garlic. Lightly simmer until butter is melted and garlic is lightly browned. In a mixer (or by hand), mix potatoes with garlic butter adding the milk slowly until desired consistency. Season with salt and pepper. (See color plate 14 for illustration.)

Sherry Gore, Pinecraft, Florida

Creamed Peas

1 (16 – 20 ounce) bag frozen peas
3 tablespoons butter
3 tablespoons flour
¼ teaspoon salt

⅛ teaspoon black or red pepper
1 cup milk
2 tablespoons Dijon mustard
(optional)

Cook peas according to package directions. In saucepan, melt butter and whisk in flour until thoroughly blended. Cook 2 minutes, stirring often. Add salt and pepper, and whisk in milk. Cook 2 minutes longer, stirring all the while. When sauce is good and thick, gently add peas, Dijon mustard (if desired), and any other vegetables you might want to add. Cook an additional 3 – 5 minutes and remove from heat. Serve hot. Note: Cooked carrots or frozen pearl onions may be added for variation.

Shannon Torkelson, Alberta, Canada

Rebecca Fisher's Sauerkraut

This Pennsylvania Dutch dish is traditionally eaten on New Year's Day. Our community celebrates the holiday at the Pinecraft Park with a sauerkraut and sausage supper. Most like it served over a mound of creamy mashed potatoes.

1 head cabbage	1 tablespoon salt (per quart)

Shred cabbage and pack loosely in jars. Make a hole down through the middle with a wooden spoon. Add a tablespoon of salt to each quart. Fill jars with boiling water and seal jars real tight. It will be ready to eat in 6 weeks. More salt may be added if desired. (See color plate 16 for illustration.)

Sherry Gore, Pinecraft, Florida

Oodles of Noodles
Thanksgiving Day, 2009

Opening an ice-cream bucket containing a pound of homemade noodles from my friend Irma brought back a flood of memories on my birthday last year.

Esther Schlabach and I combined our skills and joined the many other vendors who came out to sell homemade items at the Yoder's Farmer's Market. It was in the year 2000 when we worked at the market that was set up on Saturdays in Pinecraft, between the 50's Family Diner and Der Dutchman Restaurant. Even though we were under a tent, the strong sun rays would shine through, and we would get sunburned if we weren't careful to remember sunscreen.

Because it was a small venue compared to some, owner Milton Yoder was helpful in that he allowed only one vendor to sell a particular ware. I remember one lady baked homemade dog treats and sewed little hankies for dogs. Plants were a good seller, as was the fresh produce. Esther and I sold baked goods and noodles. I remember spending twelve hours in the kitchen on Thursdays and then again on Fridays, baking and wrapping the sugary goodies. This was hard on my son who was just four at the time, though he loved to come with me on market day.

Back then, I didn't have a mixer, just my worn-out, old wooden spoon. One friend of mine must have felt sorry for me; she gave me one of her bigger wooden spoons. It was brand new. She bought it to spank her children with but thought I needed it more than she did.

The kitchen gadget I couldn't do without was my new little cookie turner. It's a wooden-handled metal spatula; sharp on one side, finely serrated on the other. It was a gift from my friend and neighbor, Vin Yoder. It's so handy, probably a day hasn't gone by in ten years that I cooked at home that I didn't use it for something. I used it this morning to make my dippy eggs and this afternoon to cut our Thanksgiving pie.

I made the fruit breads, cookies, and bars on Thursdays, pies and cakes on Fridays. Esther made dozens of whoopie pies ahead of time, and spent her Fridays making fresh loaves of whole-wheat and white bread. The uncut loaves sold for $2.25 and the sliced bread went for $2.50.

Between the two of us, we baked a variety of treats. Here's just a few goodies we offered: sponge cake, dinner rolls, monster cookies, molasses crinkles, gingerbread, cherry Danish, coffee cakes, angel food cakes, sour cream cakes, blueberry and chocolate chip muffins, pumpkin pie, German chocolate cake, snickerdoodles, cherry pie, apple pie, zucchini bread, pumpkin bread, and yummy peanut butter cookies.

Esther's mother, Irma, dropped off cinnamon rolls to be sold. Esther's specialty was her scrumptious carrot cake, and I sold a lot of shoo-fly pies.

We made the homemade noodles every couple of weeks. Esther and I took turns picking up the fifteen to eighteen dozen eggs at Sutter's Egg Farm. We'd meet with our bags of flour at the Sunnyside fellowship hall kitchen. We used Gold Medal brand to make the noodles — that's the best. Separating the eggs was a task, as we used more yolks than whites. The remaining egg whites were saved and frozen, for making angel food cakes later.

We spent a lot of time mixing the ingredients in the commercial dough mixer. The flour was added one scoop at a time, until the dough completely pulled away from the sides of the mixing bowl. You knew it was done by the consistency — smooth and not at all sticky. It's a pretty stiff dough, as not a lot of water is used to make it.

After cleaning the kitchen and loading up the noodle dough, we'd head over to Esther's parents' house, Samuel Benders, on Houle Avenue. Their children were grown already, so there were a couple of empty guest rooms to dry the noodles in.

Our children, five between us at the time, thought this to be great fun. Of course with ten extra little hands in the dough, it made the work last longer, but what fun they had! I remember Esther and me chuckling to ourselves when my daughter Jacinda, ten at the time, remarked, "It sure takes a lot of people to make noodles."

Irma would have the wooden laundry racks set up in her kitchen for us to hang the dough on to dry a bit before we cut it. We'd work the stiff dough by kneading it until it was soft. This took some effort. Next, we carefully rolled chunks of dough into thick rolls and sliced off little patties with a paring knife. After several rolls of dough were cut, the patties were put through the noodle roller. When the racks were filled with drying dough, we would prep more for the roller. We took turns feeding the dough through the noodle cutter when it was dry enough. Some were medium, the size of the strings on our head coverings, but what sold best were the fine noodles. Folks like to use these for making creamy chicken and noodles, or chicken noodle soup. This is the size some young girls like to have for their covering strings (for our head coverings) these days.

The noodles were laid out to dry on sheets that were placed over the beds. It takes about two weeks for them to completely dry, so we'd meet back on another day at Irma's to weigh and bag the noodles. We sold them in half-pound and one-pound bags. The noodles can be frozen to last longer, but we only sold them fresh, for $2.50 a pound. It was a lot of hard work, but very rewarding.

Sherry Gore, Pinecraft, Florida

Sherry's Recipe for Homemade Egg Noodles

3 cups all-purpose flour
(approximately)
6 egg yolks

½ teaspoon salt
6 tablespoons water

On a clean countertop, make a well with the flour. Add egg yolks and salt to well. Make a very stiff yet workable dough. If necessary, add 1 tablespoon of water at a time to make dough more pliable. If dough is too sticky, do not add more flour; use 1 teaspoon oil. Divide the dough into 4 balls. Roll each one out, making as thin a layer as possible. Let dry about 45 minutes. Cut dough to form thin strips, about 2 inches long. Makes 1 pound noodles.

To cook: Bring 3 quarts of water to a boil. Add 1 tablespoon salt and ½ pound of the noodles. Stir frequently. After the water returns to a boil, cook for 8 – 10 minutes for thin noodles, 13 – 15 for medium, and 20 minutes for wide. Serves 4.

For an easy side dish, drop noodles into boiling beef, pork, or chicken stock. Reduce heat and cook at rolling boil for about 20 minutes. As the noodles boil, they'll make their own gravy. Season to taste. Chunks of chicken, beef, or pork may be added for a main dish.

Sherry Gore, Pinecraft, Florida

September 20, 2007
Sunnyside Amish Mennonite Church, Sarasota, Florida

Yoder's Restaurant has added some beauty this fall to Bahia Vista Street. Coming up quickly is the new gift shop, set to open before Christmastime. In the restaurant, peach pie is out and pumpkin is in. Pumpkin cream pie, pumpkin pancakes, and sweet potato fries are all favorites on the menu. New décor is going up too in the dining room, just in time for the first snowbirds to arrive on the Pioneer Trails bus.

Sherry Gore, Pinecraft, Florida

Sweet Potatoes Sweet Mash

Never walk away when using the broiler. While cooking in my home when being filmed by National Geographic Channel, I made the dreadful mistake of turning my back from the oven and my sweet potatoes caught fire!

Sherry Gore, Pinecraft, Florida

6 large sweet potatoes	2½ tablespoons butter
⅓ cup brown sugar	1 cup hot milk
1 teaspoon salt	2 cups mini marshmallows

Mash potatoes as you would white potatoes. Add sugar, salt, butter, and milk. Beat 2 minutes. Put in buttered casserole dish. Add marshmallows and brown under broiler.

Emma Hostetler, Millersburg, Ohio

May 21, 2008
Sunnyside Amish Mennonite Church, Sarasota, Florida

Out-of-town guests at our place Saturday were Steven Holbrooks of Montezuma, Georgia; Mrs. Sarah (Joe) Beiler of Bolivia and her second cousin Tim Millers; and Fern Kaufman from here. Sarah and Judith brought in a Bolivian meal consisting of Sopa de Mani (peanut soup) as the main dish. We never did see the peanuts and were told they were put through the grinder, making a creamy milk-like soup. The field corn, something new on the table for us, was brought down from a corn crib in Lobelville, Tennessee. The Bolivians, Sarah explained, traditionally eat bread with breakfast and enjoy field corn with dinner and supper. While most of us marveled at the tastiness of the exotic dishes and looked for seconds, Tim's little Chrisy stuck with familiar fare, all-American Bush's baked beans, left over from the school picnic.

Sherry Gore, Pinecraft, Florida

Meats and Main Dishes

Fried Chicken

chicken pieces

butter

flour

salt and pepper

Heat a cast iron skillet, or any other heavy type of skillet, on medium high. Add butter, about ¼ inch, melted. Coat chicken pieces with flour. Season with salt and pepper. Lay pieces in skillet, barely touching. Fry until nicely browned on one side. Turn pieces; reduce heat to medium and cover skillet. Cook 20 – 30 minutes. (See color plate 10 for illustration.)

Mrs. Sam (Katie) Yoder, Rose Hill, Virginia

January 6, 2010
Sunnyside Amish Mennonite Church, Sarasota, Florida

Minister Bill Yoder pointed out in announcements Sunday that as long as we are here, life will continue to go on, regardless of circumstances. There will always be births, deaths, and weddings. We were sad to learn then that Emma Stoltzfus, grandmother to Mrs. Stanley (Emileen) Mullet, passed away on Thursday. She was living with family in North Carolina at the time. Emma was the mother of eight, grandmother of fifty (one deceased), great-grandmother to thirty-one, and a dear friend to countless folks. Emma died on Thursday, December 24, 2009, just ten days shy of what would have been her eighty-seventh birthday on January 3.

Following was joyous news. Bill asked if there was a Richard Torkelson present. There was, and he was asked to stand up. Bill then asked, "Is there anybody you'd like to stand up with you?" Across the room, on the women's side, daughter Shannon Gore stood up. Bill went on to announce, "Richard popped the question to Shannon, and she said yes. He declared a wedding is planned this year."

Sherry Gore, Pinecraft, Florida

Creamy Chicken Gravy

¼ cup flour   ½ cup water
¾ – 1 cup milk

Pour fat from pan into bowl, leaving drippings in pan. Return 4 tablespoons fat to pan. Blend in flour. Turn heat down and simmer until gravy is smooth and bubbly. Remove from heat. Stir in milk and water. Bring to boil, stirring constantly. Boil and stir one full minute. You can add 2 drops Kitchen Bouquet for richness. Season with salt and pepper as desired.

Sherry Gore, Pinecraft, Florida

Yoder's Restaurant Chicken Stuffing Casserole

2 large potatoes, cubed
2 carrots, diced
8 ounces crushed corn bread
   stuffing

½ cup butter, melted
3 cups cooked chicken
1 can cream of celery soup
1 cup chicken broth

Preheat oven to 350°. Simmer potatoes and carrots in salted water until nearly done. In medium bowl, toss stuffing and butter. Spread half in a buttered 13x9-inch pan. Top with chicken. Combine soup, broth, and vegetables, and spread evenly over chicken. Add remaining stuffing on top. Bake uncovered 45 – 60 minutes.

Amanda Yoder, founder of Yoder's Restaurant, Pinecraft, Florida

---

[*The Pinecraft Pauper*]

Folks had their fill of ham, turkey, dressing, eggnog, and more than likely, something homemade and sugary. Excitement was in the air. Just before 3:00 p.m., spectators began lining the streets of Pinecraft in anticipation of the twentieth annual Christmas parade. This year's was the largest — if not to say the most unusual. Meeting behind Der Dutchman's Restaurant, participants began winding onto the streets of Pinecraft. James Graber's family delighted onlookers with their ice cream truck — a favorite of many — a costumed ice cream sandwich guy chucking ice cream sandwiches. Henry Detweiler's produce business, The Groves, was on hand with bushels of oranges for the crowd. Children squealed as local business representatives, riding through the streets on motorcycles, bicycle handlebars, truck beds, golf carts, and cleverly decorated trailers, threw bucket-loads of candy.

The best seats in the house were on the John Deere green solar buggy from Arthur, Illinois — Larry Yoder's two-wheel invention. It stays upright on two large buggy wheels by using a gyroscope, like a Segway. One spectator said, "If the Amish will consider this buggy, they will never need to manure out the horse stable again."

A journalist referred to the parade as having an "old-school feel," an idea folks outside the Pinecraft community view as a novelty. For those of us who live, work, and worship here, old school is everyday life.

Sherry Gore, Pinecraft, Florida

Turkey (or Chicken) Biscuit Skillet

¾ cup butter
¾ cup celery, chopped
¾ cup carrots, chopped
½ onion, chopped
1 cup potato, chopped
½ cup all-purpose flour
2 cups chicken broth
¾ teaspoon salt
1 ½ teaspoons black pepper
½ teaspoon dried or fresh dill, chopped
½ teaspoon dried or fresh sage, chopped
1 bay leaf
1½ cups heavy cream
3 cups turkey or chicken, cut into chunks
1 cup fresh or frozen peas
½ cup fresh or frozen corn niblets

Preheat oven to 375°. In a large saucepan, melt butter and then add celery, carrots, onion, and potato pieces. Sauté for about 5 – 8 minutes. Sprinkle flour over the vegetables and stir until the mixture starts to bubble in the pan. Using a large whisk, add chicken broth, stirring until the sauce is smooth. Season with salt, pepper, and spices. Heat to a simmer on stove top. Add the cream, turkey (or chicken), peas, and corn and cook on a slow simmer until the sauce is thickened. Place the filling in an extra large cast iron skillet. Top with fresh made biscuit dough and bake in oven until biscuits are browned and the filling is bubbling. You may also use the same filling recipe to make pot pie in a pie pan or casserole dish using your favorite pie dough recipe. If you make a pie, wrap the outside of your pie pan with foil to keep the crust from burning. Bake until center is almost brown, then remove foil to continue to cook the outer edges. Makes 6 generous servings. (See color plate 15 for illustration.)

Sherry Gore, Pinecraft, Florida

Turkey Stuffing ("Filling Balls")

3 large onions, chopped
4 celery ribs, chopped
⅔ cup butter, cubed
4½ cups chicken broth
2 tablespoons dried parsley (or ¼
  cup fresh)
1½ tablespoon sage seasoning
1½ teaspoons salt

¾ teaspoon pepper
¾ loaves each, day old homemade
  white and wheat bread, dried
  and cubed
2 eggs, beaten
½ pound roasted turkey,
  shredded (optional)

Sauté onions and celery in butter until tender. Transfer to a bowl. Add broth and seasonings. Stir in bread cubes, eggs, and turkey. Coat completely. Place in a greased 9x13-inch casserole dish. Bake at 350° for 35 minutes. Makes 10 – 12 servings. (See color plate 12 for illustration.)

Sherry Gore, Pinecraft, Florida

January 20, 2010
Sunnyside Amish Mennonite Church, Sarasota, Florida

The adult Sunday school was taught by Wilmer Miller, as Mel and Ann Mast were feeling under the weather. My little class of six has been filled to the brim with visiting children. It's been a challenge squeezing them all in the sewing room for Sunday school, but fun too.

Stutzman's Chili Casserole

1 quart homemade or 2 – 3 cans
  store-bought chili with beans
8 ounces cream cheese

10 medium-size flour tortillas
2 cups shredded cheese

Pour enough chili in bottom of casserole dish to coat bottom. Divide block of cream cheese into 10 parts with butter knife. Spread one block of cheese on each tortilla and fold in half. Layer tortillas in casserole dish, overlapping when necessary. Pour on remaining chili, covering tortillas. Sprinkle cheese on top and bake in oven until good and hot. Mrs. Danny (Monica) Stutzman made this supper for us on our first visit to their home. It's been a family favorite ever since. Makes 8 servings.

Sherry Gore, Pinecraft, Florida

EASY BROWN BUTTER

Use a heavy saucepan or skillet, unserrated knife, spatula, and ¼ cup butter (no substitutes).

1. Cut butter into pieces.
2. Heat butter in heavy saucepan over medium heat. Stir butter or swirl pan so butter doesn't burn.
3. Remove from heat when butter turns light brown and has a subtle, nutty aroma.

Poppy Seed Chicken

6 cups cooked, deboned chicken (small chunks)
2 cans cream of chicken soup
8 ounces cream cheese
12 ounces sour cream
2 sleeves Ritz crackers, crushed
½ cup butter, melted
2 tablespoons poppy seeds

Preheat oven to 350°. Spread chicken in bottom of 13x9-inch pan. Set aside. In a mixing bowl, mix soup, cream cheese, and sour cream. Combine cracker crumbs, butter, and poppy seeds; spread on top of casserole and bake 45 minutes. Makes 6 to 8 servings.

Mrs. Marek (Sarah) Alimowski, Northport, Florida

Macaroni and Cheese

3 tablespoons butter
¼ cup flour
1 teaspoon salt
½ teaspoon dry mustard
¼ teaspoon pepper
2½ cups milk
2 cups cheddar cheese

½ pound Velveeta
1 cup mozzarella cheese
1 (16 ounce) box elbow macaroni,
    cooked
paprika
ham (optional)

In a large saucepan, melt butter over low heat. Stir in flour, salt, mustard, and pepper until smooth; remove from heat. Slowly stir in milk until smooth. Stir constantly 10 minutes on heat until thick; take off heat. Stir in 1½ cups cheddar cheese, Velveeta cheese, and mozzarella cheese until melted. Put cooked macaroni in a greased casserole dish; pour cheese mixture over and mix well. Sprinkle paprika and leftover cheese on top. Bake at 375° 20 minutes. Ham (chunked) can be added to make this a main dish. Recipe can be reduced to half. (See color plates 10 and 17 for illustration.)

Shannon Torkelson, Alberta, Canada

Amish Church Dinner

ham and cheese slices
variety of pickles including bread
    and butter, dill, and seven-day
pickled red beets
homemade bread and butter
jelly

Amish church spread (see "Amish
    Peanut Butter" on page 62)
Amish church cookies
    (see page 155)
coffee

This dinner is served once or twice each summer after the morning service at the Pinecraft Amish Church. At Sunnyside Beachy Amish Mennonite Church we enjoy this meal once per year, usually on a Communion Sunday held in the spring and fall. (See color plate 7 for illustration.)

Sherry Gore, Pinecraft, Florida

Mock Ham Loaf

1 pound ground beef

1 egg, beaten

½ pound ground hot dogs

salt and pepper

1 cup cracker crumbs

Sauce

¾ cup brown sugar

½ teaspoon dry mustard

½ cup water

1 tablespoon vinegar

Preheat oven to 350°. Mix beef and next four ingredients (through cracker crumbs). In separate bowl mix sauce ingredients. Pour ½ of the sauce into meat. Shape into loaf. Pour the rest of the sauce on top. Bake 1 hour. Makes 6 – 8 servings.

Mary Zook, Dundee, Ohio

Mom's Amish Country Cooking
[Restaurant Review from *The Pinecraft Pauper* (ed. 7)]

I've often come to Mom's Restaurant to write my piece for *The Budget*, but it was the homemade, fried scrapple that beckoned me there in the first place. (Scrapple is a seasoned mixture of ground meat and cornmeal set in a mold and served sliced.) Someone in Pinecraft once told me Mom's was the best, so I tried it for myself. They weren't kidding. I only wish I could remember who it was that told me. I'm indebted to them. Forever. The scrapple was sliced thick, fried crisp on the outside, and so chock-full of secret seasonings on the inside, it was a meal in itself. The recipe has to be top secret because nobody makes scrapple like Mom's does.

You might not know this, but the restaurant is famous — maybe even historic — for it was here, in the back room, that the first-ever Pinecraft Writer's Presentation took place. Having usually eaten a delicious cheeseburger on each previous visit, on this occasion I ordered their dinner buffet for the first time. That was a historical moment in my life. It was January 20, but I remember it like it was yesterday. It tasted like a holiday dinner. Envision your mom telling you she'll make you anything and everything you want for dinner. All you have to do is serve yourself. No problem. There was macaroni and cheese, sweet potatoes, homemade mashed potatoes, and crispy fried chicken. And the gravy. Ah, the golden rich, creamy chicken gravy. These were perfect comfort foods.

Shepherd's Pie

2 pounds potatoes
1 tablespoon butter
1 egg, beaten
1 teaspoon salt
⅛ teaspoon pepper
2 tablespoons butter
½ cup chopped onion
¼ cup chopped green pepper

1 pound ground beef
1 teaspoon Kitchen Bouquet or
    Worcestershire sauce
2 tablespoons flour
½ teaspoon salt
½ teaspoon pepper
1 cup cold water

Preheat oven to 350°. Cook potatoes until soft; mash, and add butter, egg, salt, and pepper; blend until smooth. Meanwhile melt butter, add onion and green pepper, and cook 2 minutes; add ground beef. Add Kitchen Bouquet or Worcestershire sauce. Cook until lightly browned. Mix flour, salt, pepper, and cold water; add to meat. Cook, stirring until thickened. Put in casserole dish; top with potatoes. Sprinkle with paprika. Bake 20 minutes or until heated through. Green beans cooked or canned may be added to the meat mixture. I often made this after a company meal with leftovers. Makes 8 – 10 ½-cup servings.

Mrs. John Henry (Minnie) Schmucker, Burkesville, Kentucky

Anna's Barbecue

2 pounds ground beef	2 tablespoons brown sugar
2 tablespoons vinegar	½ teaspoon prepared mustard
¼ cup onion	1 cup ketchup
1 tablespoon Worcestershire	½ teaspoon celery
sauce	½ cup water

Mix all together in 3-quart kettle. Cook on medium 30 minutes. I use ½ teaspoon onion salt instead of onion. Serve on rolls.

Anna Musser, Manheim, Pennsylvania

March 4, 1988
Pinecraft, Florida

Last Friday marked history at our place when the new lane of Bahia Vista opened up and the traffic went rushing by "beneath our window." (Bahia Vista Street is being widened to a four-lane highway, taking our front lawn along with it.)

On February 20, Joel Heyman, a young Jewish boy, and Ann Darling of West Palm Beach, Florida, were with us for supper. Other out-of-town guests were Beverly Bowers from Indiana and Ruby Metzger from Delphos, Ohio. Aaron and Susan Fisher from Pennsylvania also stopped by.

Last Thursday evening the Edwin Miller family and Bob Rapp and Frieda Miller were here for supper.

Last Wednesday evening we went to the funeral home to view the body of Mark David Peachey, fourteen-year-old son of John and Carol Peachey, of Sarasota, who was killed in a freak accident as he was pinned between two vehicles on their farm. Memorial donations were given to Youth with a Mission in England, where the oldest son, John, is serving.

I took a tally of the attendance of the eleven Mennonite churches in the Sarasota area the third Sunday in February. The count was over 4,878. The Amish Church, included in this count, had a high attendance of 391, which was more than six of the Mennonite churches. The Pioneer Trails bus coming to Florida every week from Ohio and Indiana may account for a large number of Amish people coming to Florida.

Our son Matthias found a full-grown bobcat on the road out in the country recently. He brought it home, skinned it out, and preserved the hide.

Vera Overholt

Hand-Breaded Pork Chops and Creamy Country Gravy

2 tablespoons butter
½ cup vegetable oil
6 thick pork chops
1 cup milk or cream

2 cups all-purpose flour
salt and pepper
½ to 1 whole onion, sliced

Creamy Country Gravy

meat drippings
1 tablespoon butter
3 tablespoons all-purpose flour
   (more may be used)

1½ cups milk
   (I use hot milk)
salt and pepper

Heat cast iron skillet with butter and ¼ cup oil. Dip pork chops one at a time in bowl of milk. Dredge in flour. Season chops with salt and pepper. Place in heated pan along with onion slices. Cook until browned on each side and meat is no longer pink. Add more butter and remaining oil as needed until the last pork chop is cooked. Remove chops and onions and arrange on platter. To the drippings in pan, add butter and 3 tablespoons flour and slowly stir in 1½ cups milk. Now, take a little taste with a spoon. If it's not quite perfect, add more salt and pepper. That's all the spices needed for this pork chop dinner that has long been the favorite in our home. The only thing that makes this dish better is to serve with homemade creamy, red-skinned mashed potatoes (see recipe on page 100). (See color plate 14 for illustration.)

Sherry Gore, Pinecraft, Florida

Ham and Cheese Delight

½ cup finely chopped onion
1 tablespoon butter or margarine
2 cups finely chopped ham,
   cooked
1 cup shredded American cheese

3 eggs, slightly beaten
dash of pepper
1½ cups milk
⅔ cup finely crushed crackers

Preheat oven to 350°. Cook onion in butter until tender, but not brown. Combine with remaining ingredients and mix well. Bake 45 – 50 minutes or until a knife comes out clean. Makes 4 – 6 servings.

Katie E. Graber, Arthur, Illinois

Super Bowl Stromboli

6 slices Swiss cheese
2 tablespoons pizza sauce or
   mustard

6 slices salami
1 egg, lightly beaten
6 slices ham

Dough

2½ – 3 cups flour
1 tablespoon yeast
1 tablespoon sugar

1 cup warm water
1 tablespoon butter

Preheat oven to 400°. In a large bowl mix 1½ cups flour, yeast, and sugar. Heat the water and butter. Add to the dry ingredients and mix until moistened. Stir in as much of the remaining flour as is needed to form a soft dough. Turn out onto a floured surface and knead until smooth and elastic. Place into a greased bowl, flipping the dough over to grease the top. Cover and let rise in a warm place until double (about 1 hour). Punch down and turn out onto a floured surface again. Roll out into a 14x10-inch rectangle. Place on a greased baking sheet. Layer toppings down the center of dough. Spread the pizza sauce (or mustard) onto the top of the other toppings. Along each long side of the dough, cut 1-inch wide strips. Cut 2½ inches in toward the center. Start at one end alternating strips at an angle across the filling. Pinch the ends to seal. Cover and let rise until double (about 30 minutes). Brush the top with beaten egg. Bake 20 – 25 minutes. Makes 10 servings.

Mrs. Conrad (Linda) Miller, Sarasota, Florida

Tater Tot Casserole

This dish is a staple in Mennonite homes everywhere.

1 small onion	2 pounds ground beef, browned
½ cup cut up celery	2 cups peas, cooked
1 can cream of mushroom soup	1 cup shredded cheese
1 can cream of chicken soup	2 pounds tater tots

Preheat oven to 350°. Mix onion, celery, mushroom soup, and chicken soup with ground beef. Layer meat mixture in glass 13x9-inch pan. Layer peas on top, then shredded cheese. Arrange tater tots over top. Can use green beans or mixed vegetables in place of peas. Bake 35 minutes. Can make ahead. Makes 8 – 10 ½-cup servings.

Anna Musser, Manheim, Pennsylvania

Ham Loaf

2½ pounds ground ham	3 eggs, beaten
1 cup crushed saltines	2 teaspoons Lawry's seasoned salt
2½ pounds ground beef	½ cup milk
1 cup graham cracker crumbs	1½ teaspoons salt

Glaze

¾ cup brown sugar	½ tablespoon mustard
¼ cup water	¼ cup vinegar

Pineapple Sauce

1½ cups pineapple juice	1 teaspoon dry mustard
½ cup brown sugar	⅓ cup dark corn syrup
2 tablespoons unflavored gelatin	2 tablespoons vinegar

Preheat oven to 350°. In a small bowl, mix glaze ingredients. In a larger bowl combine ham and next seven ingredients (through salt) and half of glaze. Mix well and put in loaf pan. Shape into loaf like meatloaf. (It can also be baked in a roaster pan.) Bake 1 hour, basting with glaze every 15 minutes. Mix ingredients for pineapple sauce and serve over the top. For variety, shape into balls and bake on cookie sheet about 15 minutes. Serves 15–20.

Ann Mast, Sarasota, Florida

March 28, 2007
Sunnyside Amish Mennonite Church, Sarasota, Florida

No tipping, please ... Sixteen-year-old Eleanor (Wilmer) Miller was serving spaghetti at her new job and felt the plate getting too hot to handle. As she kept tipping the dish to keep her wrist from burning, she went a little too far. As if in slow motion, the spaghetti slid off the plate, landing on the table and in the lap of the shrieking customer.

Sherry Gore, Pinecraft, Florida

Spaghetti Sauce

12 ounces tomato paste
1 teaspoon sweet basil
6 ounces V – 8 juice
1 teaspoon oregano
1 pint stewed tomatoes

½ teaspoon pepper
1 clove garlic or ¼ cup ketchup
1 teaspoon garlic powder
½ cup V – 8 juice

Combine all ingredients, except ½ cup V – 8 juice, in a 6-quart stockpot, and simmer on low heat 1 hour. As it thickens, add the ½ cup V – 8 juice. Makes 8 cups.

Ruby Zehr, Goshen, Indiana

Amish Baked Hamburgers

2 pounds ground beef
3 cups bread crumbs
1 cup milk

salt and pepper to taste
1 small onion, chopped

Sauce

1 cup ketchup
½ cup sugar
2 teaspoons mustard

¾ teaspoon onion
2 teaspoons vinegar

Preheat oven to 350°. Mix beef, bread crumbs, milk, salt, pepper, and onion, and form into small patties; brown. Mix sauce ingredients and pour over patties. Bake 30 – 45 minutes. Makes 8 – 10 burgers. This is delicious served as a barbecue burger on a bun or as cutlets for a main dish.

Sherry Gore, Pinecraft, Florida

Rebecca's Tangy Meatballs

3 pounds ground beef
½ teaspoon garlic powder
1 (12 ounce) can evaporated milk
2 teaspoons salt

1 cup oatmeal
½ teaspoon pepper
1 cup cracker crumbs
2 teaspoons chili powder

Sauce

2 cups ketchup
½ teaspoon garlic powder
1 cup brown sugar

¼ cup chopped onion
½ teaspoon Liquid Smoke

Preheat oven to 350°. Combine beef and next seven ingredients (through chili powder). Form into balls and place in 13x9-inch pan. Mix sauce ingredients and spread over meatballs. Bake 1 hour. Makes 40 small (1 ounce) or 20 large (2 ounces) meatballs.

Rebecca Esh, Pinecraft, Florida

August 3, 2005
Pinecraft, Florida

Last week we had a vacation Bible school at Sunnyside. I taught the third grade with Sarah as my helper. We had a good week with quite a few children attending from non-Mennonite churches.

A lot has happened in July. Our son Nathan and our daughter Sarah both announced their engagements. A double wedding is planned for November. Nathan's fiancée is Janet Peaster from Mississippi (living in Sarasota for about two years), and Sarah's partner is Marek Alimowski from Narew, Poland. We have known the Alimowski family for about seventeen years. Marek traveled part-time with our tour groups in Europe, including our trip to Moldova. (Nathan and Hannah [our older daughter] taught English in the public school in his village.) We have not known Janet Peaster very long, but we believe she will be a real blessing in our family.

Matthias is excited! No, he is not engaged to be married, but he is engaged in caring for his new baby buffalos. Two of his water buffalos each had a calf!

On July 10, Chana Stearns and a school friend had dinner with us. They are both students at the university in Melbourne, Florida.

Alvin Troyer from Holmes County was in Sarasota for a couple weeks last month. He was helping Matthias with a small building project.

Ruxanna, from Pakistan, is in the area for a number of weeks. She has been staying with Rebecca Fisher.

The building across the street is taking on a new look. Mennonite Financial Services has moved in and is almost ready for business. They have been working a long time to renovate the building and make everything first-rate. This will be an asset for Pinecraft.

Vera Overholt

Underground Ham Casserole

4 cups cubed ham	1 cup milk
4 tablespoons butter	2 cups cheese
½ cup chopped onion	4 cups mashed potatoes
1 tablespoon Worcestershire sauce	1 pint sour cream
2 cans cream of mushroom soup	½ cup milk

Fry ham, butter, onion, and Worcestershire sauce together, and place in bottom of 8-quart roaster. In saucepan, heat mushroom soup, milk, and cheese together, and pour over ham. Mix mashed potatoes, sour cream, and milk and put on top of cheese mixture. Do not add any salt! Sprinkle with bacon bits. Bake until hot.

Mrs. John (Sadie) Esh, Burkesville, Kentucky

Yumesetti

¾ – 1 pound pork, cubed	½ cup water
1 onion, chopped	1 (10 ounce) can sliced mushrooms
vegetable oil	1 cup grated cheese
½ pound noodles	buttered bread crumbs
1 can tomato soup	

Brown pork and onions in a small amount of oil. Pour boiling water over noodles and let set for 10 minutes. Drain noodles. Mix pork, onion, noodles, tomato soup, water, and mushrooms together, and pour into casserole dish. Top with bread crumbs and grated cheese. Bake at 375° 1 hour. Serves 4 to 6 people.

Mrs. Sarah (Ralph) Schlabach

Kumm Esse!
("Come eat!")

"More" (Beef and Vegetable Casserole)

1 big onion, sliced	1 package frozen beans
1 clove garlic, minced	(10 ounces or more)
2 tablespoons butter	1 package frozen peas
2 pounds ground beef	1 package frozen corn
1 teaspoon salt	1 (20 ounce) can ripe olives, cut up
1 (28 ounce) can tomatoes	1 (4 ounce) jar pimentos, sliced
1 pound sharp cheddar cheese	2 (14 ounce) cans tomato sauce
1 pound fine noodles	Parmesan cheese, to taste

Brown onion and garlic in butter. Add beef and salt; cook until red is gone. Add tomatoes and simmer 10 minutes. Add cheddar cheese (stir until melted). Cook noodles and mix with meat. Combine beans, peas, and corn; cook until thawed and add meat. Add olives and pimentos to meat. Pour in roaster pan. Top with tomato sauce and sprinkle with Parmesan cheese. Bake at 300° 1½ hours. Serves 16–20. Serve with hot garlic bread.

Mrs. Homer (Martha) Gingerich, Pinecraft, Florida

Levi's Meatloaf

1½ pounds ground beef	⅓ cup milk
1 teaspoon salt	1 small chopped onion
1 egg, beaten	1 cup soft bread crumbs
⅛ teaspoon pepper	⅔ cup tomato juice

Topping

½ cup ketchup	1 teaspoon mustard
3 tablespoons brown sugar	

Preheat oven to 350°. Mix meatloaf ingredients, shape into a loaf, and place on a cookie sheet or in a shallow pan. Mix topping ingredients and spread over loaf. Bake 1 hour.

Mrs. Levi M. Schrock, Arthur, Illinois

March 5, 2008
Sunnyside Amish Mennonite Church, Sarasota, Florida

The youth sang at the nursing home and went on to have supper at Minister Bill Yoder's place after a presentation from Christian Aid Ministries last evening in the fellowship hall. I heard Ruth served up a tasty meal of spaghetti and ice cream for the youth, but something was missing from the table — ah, silverware! What to do? Disposable latex gloves were furnished, and Mrs. Paul (Linda) Yoder said, "Somehow P.J. came home with a clean shirt yet!"

Sherry Gore, Pinecraft, Florida

Spaghetti to Feed a Crowd

3 pounds spaghetti noodles, cooked
4½ pounds ground beef, fried
3 quarts favorite spaghetti sauce
1½ pounds Velveeta cheese, cubed
2 teaspoons salt
½ teaspoon pepper (more if you like)

Preheat oven to 325°. Drain water off noodles and add ground beef, spaghetti sauce, cheese, and seasonings. Pour into roast pan and bake 30 minutes.

Mrs. John (Mary) Fisher, Mifflin, Pennsylvania

Poor Man's Steak

2 pounds ground beef
1 cup crushed saltine crackers
1 cup water
1½ teaspoons salt
1½ teaspoons pepper
1 can cream of mushroom soup
1 cup water
flour

Preheat oven to 350°. Mix beef, crackers, water, and seasoning; put in pan and chill thoroughly or overnight. Cut into 2 – 3-inch pieces and dip in flour. Fry on both sides and place in deep baking dish so gravy won't cook over. Add mixed mushroom soup and water. Bake 1 hour.

Mrs. Levi M. Schrock, Arthur, Illinois

Scalloped Potatoes and Ham

2 cups diced ham
7 cups cooked, shredded potatoes
½ cup chopped onion
2 cups shredded cheddar cheese, divided
1 cup milk

your favorite recipe cream of mushroom soup (or 1 can)
1 cup sour cream
¼ cup butter, melted
½ teaspoon salt
black pepper to taste

Preheat oven to 350°. Mix all ingredients except 1 cup of the cheese. Put in oblong roaster and top with remaining cheese. Bake 1 hour.

Mary Miller, Zanesville, Ohio

Iowa Ham Balls

2 pounds ground beef
2 eggs, beaten
2 pounds ground ham

1½ cups milk
2 cups crushed graham crackers

Sauce

2 (10¾ ounce) cans tomato soup, undiluted
2½ cups brown sugar

2 teaspoons dry mustard
¾ cup white vinegar

Preheat oven to 350°. Combine first five ingredients; shape into balls. Place in 13x9-inch baking pan. Combine sauce ingredients and pour sauce over ham balls. Bake uncovered 1 hour.

Mrs. Lewis (Mary) Wagler, Hartville, Ohio

Applesauce Meatloaf

1 pound ground sirloin
¾ cup applesauce
½ cup bread crumbs
½ cup diced onions
2 eggs, beaten

½ teaspoon salt
¼ cup ketchup
¼ cup brown sugar, packed
2 tablespoons prepared mustard

Preheat oven to 350°. Mix ground sirloin, applesauce, bread crumbs, onions, eggs, and salt. Put in ungreased loaf pan; set aside. Combine ketchup, brown sugar, and mustard. Spread over meatloaf. Bake 1 hour. Serves 6 to 8.

Anna Wengerd, Sarasota, Florida

Sweet and Sour Meatballs

2 eggs, beaten
1 cup milk
1 cup crushed crackers

1 medium onion, chopped
1 teaspoon garlic salt
2 pounds ground beef

Sauce

1½ cup ketchup
¼ cup cider vinegar

½ cup brown sugar
¼ cup prepared mustard

Preheat oven to 350°. In a large bowl combine eggs, milk, cracker crumbs, onion, and salt. Crumble beef over mixture and mix well. Shape into 1-inch balls. In large skillet brown meatballs. Drain. Transfer into greased 3-quart baking dish. Combine sauce ingredients and pour over meatballs. Cover and bake 30 – 35 minutes. Serves 10.

Vera Kipfer, Pinecraft, Florida

If you want a hot meal, come now.
If you want a hot cook, come later.

Hot Ham and Cheese Sandwiches

4 pounds chipped ham
3 packages hamburger buns

1 pound Swiss cheese
(not sliced too thin)

Preheat oven to 350°. Use 1 slice cheese per bun. Wrap in foil and bake 15 minutes or until cheese is melted. Makes 24.

Mrs. John (Mary) Fisher, Mifflin, Pennsylvania

Hot Chicken Salad Casserole

2½ cups cooked and diced
   chicken
2 cups cooked rice
   (I use brown rice)
1 cup diced celery
1 tablespoon onion
1 can cream of chicken soup

1 teaspoon lemon juice
8 ounce can sliced water
   chestnuts
¾ cup mayonnaise
3 tablespoons butter
½ cup cornflake crumbs
½ cup slivered almonds

Preheat oven to 350°. Combine all ingredients except butter, cornflake crumbs, and almonds. Spoon into greased 2-quart casserole. Melt butter, and mix with cornflake crumbs and almonds. Put on top of casserole. Bake 30 – 45 minutes. Makes 10 – 12 ½-cup servings.

Irene Miller, Pinecraft, Florida

January 14, 2009
Sunnyside Amish Mennonite Church, Sarasota, Florida

Rainy and overcast is the word from Sarasota. I am writing this from the Ronald McDonald House in St. Petersburg. Daughter Jacinda was transported to All Children's Hospital. Her doctors are sensitive and gracious in their treatment.

Youth girls Andrea (Stanley) Mullet, Hannah (Bill) Yoder, Rebecca and Marianne Sommers, Eleanor (Wilmer) Miller, and daughter Shannon came to the hospital to sing for Jacinda. The girls looked like a breath of fresh air. Amish Henry and Sarah Detweiler, along with Eugene Miller, rode up with Mel and Ann Mast to bring lunch. Folks in the full cafeteria were astonished to see the spread they brought. Ann and Sarah made pot roast and potatoes, rich chocolate cake, and a fresh fruit salad. They even set the table with pretty linens.

Sherry Gore, Pinecraft, Florida

Chicken Pie

1 tablespoon butter
3 tablespoons flour
1 quart chicken broth
1 cup diced potatoes
1½ cups sliced carrots

1 cup diced celery
1 cup chicken, cooked and diced
3 hard-boiled eggs
1 teaspoon salt

Dough

2 cups flour
1½ teaspoons baking powder
½ cup milk

salt to taste
2 tablespoons lard

Preheat oven to 350°. Melt butter and mix with flour. Add chicken broth and cook to gravy consistency. Cook potatoes, carrots, and celery, and add to the thickened broth along with chicken and eggs. Stir in salt. Mix gently. Put into a greased casserole dish. *Dough:* Mix and roll as for pie dough, cutting slits in top. Place over chicken and vegetables in casserole. Bake 30 minutes. Makes 8 1-cup servings.

Darlene Hostetler, Coshocton, Ohio

Huntington Chicken

4 cups broth
flour, for thickening
½ cup milk
salt (to taste)
pepper (to taste)
1 quart deboned chicken
½ cup chopped onion
1 teaspoon garlic powder

2 teaspoons poultry seasoning
½ cup melted butter
½ cup chopped celery
4 more cups broth
2 cups noodles, boiled and
  drained
½ cup Velveeta, cubed
2 cups bread crumbs

Thicken boiling broth with flour and milk. Add salt and pepper. Mix the rest of the ingredients except for the bread crumbs and place in 8-quart baking dish. Spread bread crumbs on top and bake 30 minutes. Serves 12.

Mrs. Sylvanus (Mary) Hershberger, Millersburg, Ohio

Beef Stew with Dumplings

2 pounds cubed beef	1½ teaspoons salt
3 tablespoon fat (or vegetable oil)	⅛ teaspoon pepper
1 small onion, chopped	4 cups boiling water
2 tablespoons flour	1 teaspoon lemon juice

Dumplings

4 cups flour	2 cups broth of your choice
½ cup butter	1 teaspoon salt
2 teaspoons baking powder	

Cut meat into small cubes. Melt fat in a hot skillet or Dutch oven. Brown meat and onion in fat, keep it sizzling hot until nicely browned. Sprinkle flour, salt, and pepper over meat. Add the boiling water and lemon juice. Cover the pan and lower the heat so that meat simmers 3 – 3½ hours.

To make the dumplings, mix all ingredients together and drop by spoonfuls into boiling broth. Cover and allow to cook 12 – 25 minutes.

Sarah McGuire Montgomery, Indiana

Spanish Rice

2 tablespoons butter	1 cup water
½ cup dry rice	¾ teaspoon salt
½ chopped green pepper	1 (20 ounce) can tomatoes
1 onion, minced	½ teaspoon celery salt
½ – ¾ pound ground beef	⅛ teaspoon pepper

Melt butter in frying pan. Add rice, green pepper, onion, and beef. Let brown until the meat is lightly browned and the rice golden, stirring to prevent overbrowning in spots. Add water, salt, tomatoes, celery salt, and pepper. Let simmer slowly until all the liquid is absorbed and the rice is tender, about 30 minutes.

Mrs. Dean (Edna) Hochstetler

October 29, 2008
Sunnyside Amish Mennonite Church, Sarasota, Florida

Mrs. Paul (Linda) Yoder told me this morning there were quite a few visitors in church as two motor homes pulled in carrying twenty folks from the Cuba Mennonite group in Indiana. "How many of them were Cuban?" I asked with interest. "Oh, none of them!" she said. The encyclopedia says that Cuba, an unincorporated town, was named in honor of veterans in the Spanish-American War. It is also home to Cuba Mennonite School. Their mission this week is to help out at Gator Wilderness Boys Camp. "Our young people try and do a voluntary service workweek like this once a year," Pastor James Miller told the congregation as he delivered the main message in church.

Sherry Gore, Pinecraft, Florida

Marinating Sauce for Chicken

¼ teaspoon pepper
½ teaspoon Accent
½ teaspoon garlic powder
2 tablespoons water

1 tablespoon brown sugar
¼ cup soy sauce
1 tablespoon vegetable oil

Combine all ingredients. Place cut up chicken in gallon Ziploc bag and add marinade. Turn frequently.

Mrs. Levi M. Schrock, Arthur, Illinois

Supper, supper what to make?
Chicken's thawed, but I want cake.
Kriste Wolfe

MAKING GOOD GRAVY

Place one tablespoon of butter in a small saucepan over medium heat, and add ¼ cup of white flour. Stir while cooking. The length of cooking time depends on personal taste. The longer the mixture cooks, the darker your roux will turn out as butter browns.

When desired color is achieved, add one full cup of beef or chicken stock while whisking vigorously. Remove from heat.

The temperature of the stock makes no difference. Just pour it all in and whisk to your heart's content. Return the pan to the stove and bring stock to a boil.

Cook gravy for at least 2 additional minutes. Turn the burner down and simmer on low. A skin will form on your gravy if you leave the pan uncovered.

September 17, 2008
Sunnyside Amish Mennonite Church, Sarasota, Florida

Visions of cool autumn weather are quickly squelched as soon as you step outside. It's still sizzling here. Family friends Mike and Richard Torkelson flew in from northern Alberta, Canada, and stayed with their grandmother, Martha Gingerich, in Pinecraft. Richard was shocked at the intense heat as he stepped out the door at the airport. He took his previous trip here in February when the weather was glorious. Several visits out to swim at Siesta Key Beach made the heat more bearable.

The Bill Yoders hosted the youth at their place and invited the youth's families over for a night of sloppy Joes and old-fashioned games most of the youth had never played. It was a full house with Danita Troyer, new teacher Rachel Yoder, and the Torkelson boys along for the activities.

Sherry Gore, Pinecraft, Florida

My Favorite Sloppy Joes

1 pound lean ground beef
¼ cup chopped onion
¼ cup chopped green bell pepper
1 teaspoon prepared yellow
    mustard

½ teaspoon garlic powder
salt and pepper to taste
¾ cup ketchup
3 teaspoons brown sugar

Fry ground beef with onions and green pepper. Drain fat. Stir in remaining ingredients. Simmer 30 minutes or so. Quick and easy supper when served on hamburger buns with potato chips on the side. Makes 6 servings.

Sherry Gore, Pinecraft, Florida

October 22, 2008
Sunnyside Amish Mennonite Church, Sarasota, Florida

Twenty ladies from church turned out at Troyer's Restaurant in Pinecraft Friday to help Laura Yoder celebrate her eighty-seventh birthday. Stamps, stationery, and gift certificates were among the practical gifts she received, with a certificate for Chinese food being among her favorites.

Laura shared her life story with the schoolchildren recently. Born in 1921, Laura's wages were $8 per week (including room and board) at age twenty-one, for working on a Mennonite couple's farm. Her duties included milking five to six cows every morning and evening and helping to butcher forty to sixty chickens every Friday for the farmers' market on Saturday. On holidays, when the couple would butcher chickens, ducks, geese, and turkeys, it was Laura's job to cut off their heads with a sharp knife, though, she said, "I never cut the head off a turkey." She said a good pair of shoes could be bought for $2 a pair. Laura's best advice to the children was "to do voluntary service before you get married." Laura (Miss Helmuth) married widower Henry J. Yoder just two days shy of her fortieth birthday, on October 15, 1961.

Sherry Gore, Pinecraft, Florida

Amish-Style Chinese Chop Suey

2 pounds ground beef
1 cup chopped onion
1 can cream of mushroom soup
1½ cups chopped celery
1 can cream of chicken soup
3 cups water

2 teaspoons salt and pepper mix
1 cup uncooked rice
1 bag chow mein noodles
buttered bread crumbs
  for topping

Preheat oven to 300°. Brown ground beef and onion, then combine all ingredients except chow mein noodles and bread crumbs. Put in greased baking dish and top with crumbs. Bake 1½ – 2 hours. Sprinkle chow mein noodles on top last 10 minutes.

Sarah Joy Beiler, Sarasota, Florida

December 17, 2008
Sunnyside Amish Mennonite Church, Sarasota, Florida

Hopefully the rain will hold back for tonight's fund-raiser supper for the Haiti Benefit Auction coming up. Amish Henry Detweiler will be out at the Pinecraft Park with his kettle, cooking up ground beef — haystacks are on the menu.

Sherry Gore, Pinecraft, Florida

Mrs. Paul (Linda) Yoder's sisters-in-law, Grace and Ella, remember
in their youth a boy cousin of about nine or so who asked them,
"How come we always sing 'Amazing Grace' and not 'Amazing Ella'?"

Favorite Haystack Meal

crumbled taco chips

1 large onion, chopped and fried with 2 pounds ground beef meat

1½ quarts cooked rice (we prefer brown rice)

1 quart cooked navy or pinto beans (or both)

1 quart cheese sauce to ladle over the above ingredients

1 large head lettuce

2 cups diced tomato

2 cups diced bell pepper

2 cups diced onion

shredded cheese on top (if desired)

Place each ingredient in its own bowl. Start with taco chips and each one builds their own haystack on their plate in order given and top with dressing. Makes 10 – 12 servings.

Sherry Gore, Pinecraft, Florida

Dressing

2 cups mayonnaise

⅓ cup sugar (or honey)

1 tablespoon prepared mustard

⅓ teaspoon celery seed

Combine all ingredients until smooth.

Mrs. John (Sadie) Esh, Burkesville, Kentucky

Pan-Fried Chicken

1 (3½ pound) fryer

2 teaspoons salt

⅛ teaspoon pepper

⅓ cup flour

Preheat oven to 325°. Cut chicken into serving pieces. Wash chicken. Drain, but do not wipe dry. Sprinkle with salt and pepper mixture. Place flour in a paper bag, add chicken pieces, and shake bag until chicken is well covered. Melt fat to a depth of ½ inch in a heavy skillet. When fat is moderately hot, add chicken pieces; do not crowd. Turn the pieces to brown on all sides. If a crisp crust is desired, cover pan for the first half of cooking period, then uncover. If a tender crust is desired, brown pieces with pan uncovered and then remove them to rack in roasting pan. Cover and bake 1 hour. Serves 6 – 8.

Vera Kipfer, Pinecraft, Florida

October 29, 2008
Sunnyside Amish Mennonite Church, Sarasota, Florida

Daughter Shannon hosted a "Thank You" dinner here at home yesterday for several Sunday school teachers. Trying her hand at cooking for a crowd, she spent two and a half days preparing chicken and dumplings and many other tempting goodies. Among the twenty-four guests were the Nathan Overholts, the Tim Yoders, Sarah Joy, Tim and Kevin Beiler, all of the youth, and some younger siblings. Friends Cathy and Leah from Yoder's Restaurant were present as well.

Sherry Gore, Pinecraft, Florida

Chicken and Dumplings

Drop a whole chicken into your biggest stockpot of boiling water. Chicken parts are okay too, just not as much fun. Add some salt and pepper. It's going to be a while, so go catch up on chores or read the latest copy of *The Budget* while you wait. Remove the chicken when it starts to fall off the bone. Don't try and debone it yet; it's hot! Let it cool some. You could read some more, or you could chop up some vegetables for your stew. It's a good way to stretch your dinner in case company drops in. Potatoes, carrots, onions — whatever you like. Early peas are good too. Turn broth down to simmer and add a little butter. The fat is where the flavor is. Add some roux to the broth if you like a thicker stew. Cream of chicken soup will do in a pinch as well. When you have the chicken all picked, return it to the broth and let it simmer. Throw out the bones.

About ½ hour before you're ready to eat, turn the heat up and make the dumplings by mixing 2 cups baking mix (Bisquick) with ⅔ cup milk. Drop by heaping spoonfuls into boiling stew. Cook dumplings uncovered 10 minutes. Cover your pot and cook 10 additional minutes. Don't peek; just let them steam. Ladle stew into individual bowls. You might think you're ready to eat, but it's best to let it cool off some. Dumplings hold enough steam inside to keep the stew hot for you to come back for seconds.

Growing up, we would eat our chicken and dumplings over cooked noodles or rice. We liked ours pretty peppery too. Some folks I know pour it over a mound of mashed potatoes; there's no wrong way to do it. I haven't met a pot of dumplings I didn't like.

Sherry Gore, Pinecraft, Florida

May 7, 2008
Sunnyside Amish Mennonite Church, Sarasota, Florida

Bill Yoder had several folks over for dinner, and Kris Knepp shared of their courtship days. With Rebecca going off to the Dominican Republic for two years rather than one, Kris told us, "If Jacob waited seven years for the wrong girl, then I can wait two years for the right one!" Rebecca's father said to him, "You know, I do have an older daughter."

Sherry Gore

Seafood

Shrimp and Grits

2 cups water	4 slices bacon, finely diced
2 cups milk	2 cloves garlic, finely minced
1 teaspoon Old Bay seasoning	1 large onion, chopped
4 cloves garlic, finely diced or minced	1 tablespoon flour
	1 pound pink Gulf shrimp
3 tablespoons butter	¾ cup water, divided
1 cup stone-ground grits	½ teaspoon Old Bay seasoning
2 tablespoons butter	2 teaspoons vegetable bouillon

Heat water, milk, Old Bay, garlic, and 3 tablespoons butter to almost boiling in medium saucepan. Add grits and cook 6 – 8 minutes, stirring occasionally. Meanwhile, in separate skillet, melt 2 tablespoons butter and sauté bacon, garlic, and onion. When lightly browned, add flour and make a basic roux. Stir until fully blended. Add shrimp and ¼ cup water. Cover and simmer. When shrimp are partially cooked, add ½ cup water, ½ teaspoon Old Bay, and bouillon. Simmer until gravy thickens. Serve grits with shrimp and gravy. This makes a delicious dish for brunch or supper. Makes 5 – 7 servings.

Sherry Gore, Pinecraft, Florida

Grouper Marinade

1 onion, thinly sliced	¼ cup lemon juice
½ cup butter, melted	1 tablespoon barbecue sauce

Salt and pepper the fish. Spread onion slices over fish. Pour sauce mixture of butter, lemon juice, and barbecue sauce over fish and marinade at least 2 hours. Grill or bake.

Mary Ellen Mullet, Nappanee, Indiana

GO FISHING! FREEZE YOUR CATCH

Wash fish with cold running water until water runs clear. Dry with paper towels and wrap in plastic. Store in freezer bags for best results. Fish keeps in the freezer six months or in the refrigerator one day when thawed.

TIP

Is It Fresh?

When purchasing fish at the market, whole fish should have bright clear eyes. Look for shiny, clean-looking fish. Avoid fish that have discolored patches or are dull looking. The gills should be bright red not dull colored. Fresh fish should smell like clean water not yesterday's catch. If it smells fishy, don't buy it! If there's a milky liquid on the fish, run, don't walk. This is a sure sign of rotting fish.

Thawing

Thaw seafood in the refrigerator overnight. Avoid thawing on the counter. Cook immediately after thawing. Never refreeze.

Quick and Spicy Fish Fillets

6 finely textured fish fillets, such as flounder, sole, or cod
1 egg, beaten
½ cup grated Parmesan cheese
½ cup cornflake crumbs
¼ teaspoon ground red pepper (optional)

Heat oven to 450°. Dip fish in egg. Coat with combined cheese, crumbs, and pepper. Place in greased shallow baking dish. Bake 5 – 10 minutes or until fish flakes easily with fork. Makes 6 servings.

Mrs. Sam (Katie) Yoder, Rose Hill, Virginia

March 12, 2006
Sunnyside Amish Mennonite Church, Sarasota, Florida

I see the temperature outside is 88 degrees, which feels like summer already. This morning when I looked outside, I also noticed that it looked like summer because of how green the trees were. Seems like it happened overnight that the trees got their real beautiful dark green color leaves back with their new summer look.

Yesterday was a busy and interesting day for us. We had a craft fair and did well, and a few came home sunburned since this was an outside setup. This coming weekend will be Pinecraft Days in downtown Amish country, a three-day setup.

David Schlabach had the misfortune of the ladder step he was standing on while picking oranges break, causing him to land on the ground and break his wrist. So he is off work with his wrist in a cast.

N. Miller

Clam Chowder

Dad was raised on Buzzard's Bay, near Cape Cod, Massachusetts. His mother ran a tearoom out of Eagle Hill, their farm. This was one of Dad's favorite dishes.

4 dozen hard-shell clams, scrubbed, or 1 quart shucked cooked clams with their broth
6 slices bacon (or ¼ pound diced salt pork)
1 onion, coarsely chopped
6 medium potatoes, peeled and cut into ½-inch cubes
2 cups milk
2 cups half-and-half or evaporated milk
6 tablespoons unsalted butter
salt and pepper to taste

Pour clams into a large pot with one cup water. Cover, bring to a boil, and cook until shells open, about 10 minutes. Allow to cool, then shuck clams and set aside. Pour off broth and reserve, but let the gritty residue stay on the bottom of the pan. Cook bacon in a large saucepan over medium heat. Add onion and cook, stirring, until tender. Pour off half the fat. Add potatoes to the pan and stir well. Add clam broth and just enough water to cover the potatoes. Simmer until potatoes are tender. Add milk and half-and-half; bring to a simmer. Add clams and butter; simmer a few minutes until clams are heated through and butter is melted. (Do not boil or clams will be tough! Trust me on that.) Season with salt and pepper.

Suzanne Woods Fisher, San Francisco, California

Peppered Lime Batter for Fish

juice of 3 key limes, squeezed
2 egg whites
1½ cups flour
¾ cup water
1 teaspoon baking soda
black pepper to taste
⅛ teaspoon salt

Makes enough batter for 2 pounds fillets. Mix ingredients well. Pat fish dry with paper towels before dipping in batter. Fry fish until golden brown.

Sherry Gore, Pinecraft, Florida

Instead of Frying Fish

1 pound walleye, perch, or pike
   fillets
¼ cup milk
1 cup crushed potato chips
¼ cup grated Parmesan cheese
¼ teaspoon dried thyme
1 tablespoon dry bread crumbs
2 tablespoons butter

Preheat oven to 450°. Cut fish into serving-size pieces. Place milk in shallow bowl. In another bowl, combine potato chips, Parmesan cheese, and thyme. Dip fish in milk, then coat with the chip mixture. Sprinkle a greased 8-inch square baking dish with bread crumbs. Place fillets over crumbs and drizzle with butter. Bake uncovered 12 – 14 minutes, or until fish flakes with a fork. Makes 4 servings.

Barbara Yoder, Colon, Michigan

October 13, 2008
Sunnyside Amish Mennonite Church, Sarasota, Florida

Minister Bill Yoder took the boys to Venice Beach Saturday on a shark tooth excursion. With the water over their necks, the boys swam out to the sandbar in hopes of finding the really big teeth. Later several fellows came out armed with huge fishing poles as it turned to dusk. Ripe with curiosity, one boy asked, "Whatcha fishing for?" One man gently scolded and said, "You boys really shouldn't be out here this late. Didn't you know there's sharks, and that's a feeding frenzy out there?" he said, pointing toward the bait fish flying up out of the water. The boys headed back inland and spent the rest of their time by shore using their sifters to find teeth and throwing cast nets to catch jack fish.

Sherry Gore, Pinecraft, Florida

Oyster Stew

2 (10 ounce) oysters	½ cup butter
½ cup finely diced carrots	1½ teaspoons salt
½ cup finely diced celery	2 tablespoons flour
4 cups milk	1 teaspoon Worcestershire sauce

Combine ingredients and heat thoroughly. After soup is hot, let set 15 minutes to get the fullest flavor. Makes 4 – 6 servings.

Susan Fisher, Pinecraft, Florida

Nothing makes a fish bigger
than almost being caught.

Escalloped Oysters

½ cup soft bread crumbs
1 cup cracker crumbs
2 cups oysters
6 tablespoons butter

⅛ teaspoon pepper
¼ cup milk or cream
salt to taste

Preheat oven to 400°. Grease a baking dish. Arrange a layer of the combined bread and cracker crumbs in bottom of dish. Add a layer of oysters. Dot oysters with butter. Add salt and pepper. Repeat leaving a layer of crumbs on top; dot with small pieces of butter. Have only 2 layers of oysters. Moisten with milk and oyster liquid combined. Bake 30 minutes. Serve at once. Makes 6 servings.

Mrs. Sylvanus (Mary) Hershberger, Millersburg, Ohio

January 21, 2009
Sunnyside Amish Mennonite Church, Sarasota, Florida

The schoolchildren were excited to see Matthias Overholt grade the driveway after filling it with a coating of new shell. Seashells are not only cheaper than gravel, but among the broken shells are also thousands of petrified shark teeth.

I am writing this once again from the Ronald McDonald House in St. Petersburg. Things were touch and go for several days, but [my daughter] Jacinda is finally stable, and we hope to go home sometime early this week. Daughter Shannon sat with her yesterday so I was able to be in church.

Sisters sewing was Wednesday. The Haiti quilt made with the labor of love came within one day of completion. Laura Yoder and Mrs. (Emanuel) Fannie Yoder, along with some others, worked on Thursday to have the quilt ready for Saturday's Haiti benefit auction.

Sherry Gore, Pinecraft, Florida

Seafood Chowder

2½ cups diced potatoes

2 cups carrots, chopped

1 cup celery, chopped

1 cup onion, diced

4 cups water

1 pound imitation crab meat

1 pound shrimp (can be less)

4 teaspoons chicken base

½ cup butter (no imitations)

¾ cup all-purpose flour

2 cups half and half

2 cups milk

salt and pepper

Old Bay Seasoning

Using large stockpot, cook first 4 ingredients (through onion) in 4 cups water until soft. Add crab, shrimp, and chicken base. In separate pan melt butter. Stir in flour, half and half, and milk. Cook on medium to medium-low heat until thickened. Add to first mixture. Sprinkle with seasonings to taste. (See color plate 11 for illustration.)

Mrs. Bill (Ruth) Gingerich, Sarasota, Florida

November 9, 2009

Sunnyside Amish Mennonite Church, Sarasota, Florida

Son Tyler has had pretty good success fishing the last couple of years in Pinecraft Park. Just last week he reeled in a 31-inch tarpon, which he released. Not everything he's hooked has been good so far. The other day he reminded me why he doesn't regret his decision to forgo swimming in Philippi Creek.

Some months back he chose to stay out of the water after sighting an enormous gar fish, a species known for its nasty teeth and aggressiveness. Several boys would often swim just downstream a bit from the boat ramp, where someone had fastened a rope to a tree to swing out from it and drop. The other day, Tyler cast his line out into the water in that very spot and was dismayed to pull up a discarded pickax. Some catches make better dinner than others.

Sherry Gore, Pinecraft, Florida

Savory Fish Fillets

1 pound frozen flounder
1 can cream of celery soup

½ cup shredded cheddar cheese
paprika

Preheat oven to 350°. Thaw fish in large bowl of cold water. Blot dry on paper towels. In shallow greased baking dish, arrange one layer of fish. Pour soup over top and spread on evenly. Top with cheese and sprinkle with paprika. Bake 15 minutes or until fish flakes easily with fork.

Mrs. Sylvanus (Mary) Hershberger, Millersburg, Ohio

September 26, 2000
Pinecraft, Florida

Several weeks ago, Rick Knepp and others went fishing for shark in our Sarasota waters. Rick caught a huge shark, eight feet long, just about a hundred yards off South Lido Beach. The fishermen fought it for several hours. They dragged it back to the dock because it was too big and heavy to lift into the boat. Rick brought it by for us to see, and son Matthias cut it up for the freezer. Now we have shark steaks on the menu. Call us if you want to have a piece, or perhaps you would rather have alligator meat?

Vera Overholt

Fabulous Grilled Fish and Shrimp Dinner

1 pound fillets of sole
1½ pounds cleaned, raw Gulf shrimp, fresh or frozen
1 teaspoon salt
½ – ¾ cup sliced mushrooms
2 tablespoons butter
1 cup dry cooking sherry

2 teaspoons dehydrated minced onion
1 tablespoon cornstarch or Clear Jel
⅓ cup water
2 tablespoons lemon juice

Thaw fillets and shrimp in cold water if frozen. Divide into 4 portions; sprinkle each with ¼ teaspoon salt. In small pan, cook mushrooms in butter until tender, but not browned; stir in sherry and onion. Mix cornstarch (or Clear Jel) and water until smooth; stir into mushroom mixture. Cook, stirring constantly, until mixture thickens and boils; boil and stir 1 minute. Stir in lemon juice. Place one portion fish on each of four 14x10-inch pieces of heavy-duty foil. Place ¼ of shrimp on each. Turn up foil. Spoon mushrooms sauce over shrimp. Wrap securely in heavy-duty aluminum foil. Place foil packets on grill 4 inches from medium coals. Cook 20 minutes or until fish flakes easily with fork. Delightful dinner when served with jasmine rice and cooked carrots and cauliflower on the side. Makes 4 servings.

Mrs. Sylvanus (Mary) Hershberger, Millersburg, Ohio

GRILLING SEAFOOD

A grill basket works great for cooking whole fish, including snapper, trout, and salmon. Delicate fish, such as flounder, catfish, or perch fillets, do best in the basket too. Hearty tuna, shark, and swordfish steaks are fantastic when cooked directly on the grill. Brush fish lightly with oil to prevent sticking when grilling directly on the rack.

One easy way to grill is to cook on a large sheet of aluminum foil. Fish can also be grilled by wrapping in a foil pouch. Use a nonstick spray or oil lightly.

Experiment with different herbs, spices, and seasonings to find your niche. Cajun seasoning, lemon pepper, and Old Bay seasoning are Floridian favorites.

Always grill fillets over medium to medium-low heat. Turn fish only once. Fish should flake easily and be opaque-colored when ready to eat. Never close the grill lid when cooking. Too much smoke will affect the flavor.

Scallops and shrimp do best on skewers. Soak wooden skewers before grilling or use metal.

Keep marinating fish in the refrigerator. Always use fresh marinade when ready to grill. Discard any leftover juice to avoid bacteria.

Place clams, lobster, mussels, and oysters directly over the hottest coals. Shellfish is ready when the shell is open. Use the 5-minute rule; pitch any that don't open quickly.

Golden Catfish Fillets

1 egg white	¼ – ½ teaspoon cayenne pepper
1 cup milk	⅛ teaspoon pepper
1 cup cornmeal	4 catfish fillets (8 ounces each)
¾ teaspoon salt	cooking oil
¼ teaspoon garlic powder	lemon or lime wedges, optional

In shallow bowl, beat egg white until foamy; add milk and mix well. In another shallow bowl, combine cornmeal, salt, garlic powder, cayenne, and pepper. Dip fillets in milk mixture, then coat with cornmeal mixture. Heat ¼ inch of oil in a large skillet. Fry fish over medium-high heat 3 – 4 minutes per side or until it flakes easily with a fork. Garnish with lemon or lime if desired. Makes 4 servings.

Esther Martin, Martinsburg, Pennsylvania

BAKING SEAFOOD

Fillets, steaks, whole fish, and shellfish taste delicious when baked in a very hot oven. Spray baking sheet with nonstick spray or oil lightly. Place fish skin-side down in pan. Cook 10 minutes at 450° for each inch of thickness. Turn whole fillets or steaks one time halfway through baking. Remember, seafood will be opaque when ready to eat. Add 5 minutes to cooking time when cooking with sauce or aluminum foil. Fresh sliced lemon or bottled lemon juice adds great flavor to mild fish fillets such as whiting.

TIP

PAN FRYING SEAFOOD

Use a sturdy heavy-duty skillet to fry fish. Avoid cooking too many pieces of fish at once, as this lowers the temperature of the oil, compromising the texture and taste of the fish. When cooking large quantities of fish, keep in a warm oven until ready to serve. When using breading such as cornmeal, store breaded fish in refrigerator 15 – 20 minutes first to ensure the breading will stick to the fish instead of the pan. Allow 4 minutes per side for deep frying batter-dipped fish.

TIP

April 30, 2007
Sunnyside Amish Mennonite Church, Sarasota, Florida

At the annual church picnic at Myakka River State Park Saturday, Lester Hostetler reported seeing a wild boar sow with her thirteen to fourteen piglets roaming the grounds. Lester, Stanley Mullet, and Wilmer Miller were up at 6:00 a.m. grilling the chicken the rest of us were treated to for lunch. Joining the picnic with my family were Perry and Lois Yoder, our company from North Carolina. Their six little children kept us on our toes with their giggles and smiles all weekend. It was refreshing for my daughter Jacinda to have them here, as their smiles and laughter were contagious and took her mind off her upcoming surgery tomorrow.

Not everyone's day ended calmly. Son Tyler (twelve) had a harrowing gator experience while at the church picnic. As he slowly approached our table with a white face and weakly said, "Mom," several of us knew something was amiss but thought he was perhaps just in need of water from being overheated. "No, Mom, I almost got eaten by an alligator."

We sat him down and listened to his hoarse account of what happened, that caused him and Gideon (Frank) Keifer (thirteen) to scream from being so frightened while fishing for largemouth bass. Deacon Perry Miller, who was at the water's edge, too, chronicled the events like this:

"Tyler was standing on an unstable stump in the water. The last time, as he cast his line out, it dropped four feet in front of him. Unbeknownst to Tyler, it apparently startled the lurking alligator lying at the bottom of the river, just below where he was standing. The alligator exploded out of the water, its entire head and tail up in the air and going down with a terrific splash. Tyler almost lost his footing as he teetered on that stump, trying to keep his balance."

Brother Perry told us he didn't think the alligator was trying to eat Tyler but noted that it was "a thirteen-foot monster."

Sherry Gore, Pinecraft, Florida

Alligator Stew

1 pound cut up alligator meat
½ cup vegetable oil
½ cup chopped onion
½ cup chopped celery
½ cup chopped bell pepper
2 tablespoons minced parsley
1 (10 ounce) can Rotel or other brand tomatoes with green chilies
salt and pepper
1 cup cooked brown or white rice

Place gator meat and cooking oil in a stockpot. Cover with chopped up vegetables, parsley, tomatoes, and chilies. Season with salt and pepper. Cover and cook over medium to medium-low heat for an hour or more. Cook rice while stew simmers. Ladle stew over bowls of hot, cooked rice. Good with a few shakes of hot pepper sauce too. Makes 4 generous servings.

Sherry Gore, Pinecraft, Florida

October 20, 2004
Pinecraft, Florida

I just got out of the hospital a week ago today. I was in for a week with heart-related problems. A person really learns to appreciate family and friends and the extended family of the church in times like these.

The other Saturday before my hospital stay, I went out to Nathan and Matthias's place on Richardson Road for dinner. The special occasion was a meal for all of Nathan's workers in his lawn maintenance and landscaping business. The special food on the menu was alligator meat. It was delicious. Nathan had caught the alligator that we ate and also had a large (eight feet or more) alligator wrapped in ice that he had just caught the night before.

Vera Overholt

Grilled Lime Fish Fillets

2 pounds frozen fish fillets,
   thawed
canola oil
paprika

½ cup butter
¼ cup lime juice
salt and pepper

Brush fish with oil and sprinkle with paprika. Place fish in hinged grill basket or on well-greased grill 3 – 4 inches from medium coals. Cook 5 to 7 minutes on each side or until fish flakes easily with fork, basting frequently with mixture of butter and lime juice. Just before serving, sprinkle with salt and pepper. Serve with fresh lime wedges, and white or wild rice.

For bacon-wrapped fillets: Before placing fish on grill, place lime slices on side of fish; wrap fish and lime slices with bacon slices. Secure bacon with toothpicks. (See color plate 18 for illustration.)

Sherry Gore, Pinecraft, Florida

October 24, 2007
Sunnyside Amish Mennonite Church, Sarasota, Florida

Stone crab season starts today in Sarasota, but expect to pay $25 per pound to enjoy this popular seafood. Four years ago, while working for State Senator Lisa Carlton, I was treated to a five-pound bag of stone crab claws, which I saved to eat with Jerry and Joanna Williams in Burkesville, Kentucky.

I still remember the laughter at the table and the looks on the smiling children's faces when they cracked open their supper with a hammer.

Sherry Gore, Pinecraft, Florida

Shrimp Scampi

2 pounds jumbo shrimp, fresh or
frozen
½ cup butter, melted
1 tablespoon fresh parsley,
chopped

⅛ teaspoon Lawry's seasoned salt
1 tablespoon paprika
⅛ teaspoon red pepper
2 cloves minced garlic
¼ cup white wine vinegar

Thaw and pat dry shrimp. Melt butter in saucepan or microwave. Add seasonings and vinegar and stir. Combine shrimp and butter mixture in baking pan. Bake in preheated oven at 500° 7 – 8 minutes. Do not overbake. Makes 6 servings.

Mrs. John (Ruth) Gingerich, Sarasota, Florida

You never know how many friends you have until you rent a house on the beach.

Cookies and Bars

Amish Church Cookies

These cookies are traditionally served to small children in the middle of a church service that lasts several hours.

5 – 6 cups flour, plus more for rolling out dough
1½ teaspoons baking soda
2½ teaspoons baking powder
½ teaspoon salt

1½ cups shortening, softened
2½ cups sugar
3 large eggs
1¼ cups whole milk
1½ teaspoons vanilla

Preheat oven to 375°. Sift together flour, baking soda, baking powder, and salt in large bowl. In a separate bowl, cream together shortening and sugar until light and fluffy. Add eggs one at a time. Add milk and vanilla. Add dry ingredients and mix until a soft dough forms (add extra flour if needed to get soft). Roll out dough on lightly floured surface to ½-inch thickness. Cut with round cookie cutter. Place on baking sheet lined with parchment and bake 10 – 12 minutes until edges just begin to turn golden. Allow to cool and frost with Church Cookie Frosting (next recipe). Makes 3 dozen 4-inch cookies.

Sherry Gore, Pinecraft, Florida

Church Cookie Frosting

3½ cups powdered sugar   ½ cup milk
½ cup shortening   ½ teaspoon vanilla

Combine all ingredients together in bowl and mix until smooth and creamy. Food coloring and extra flavoring may be added.

Sherry Gore, Pinecraft, Florida

February 28, 2007
Sunnyside Amish Mennonite Church, Sarasota, Florida

The fifteenth annual Pinecraft Days started Thursday. Esther Schlabach and her mother, Irma Bender, had their delicious bakery items for sale, and Mrs. Thomas (Leah) Peachey, along with her sister, Mary Miller, had quilt tops for sale in front of Thomas's Big Olaf ice cream store. Grace Yoder from Sarasota Mennonite Church is still selling Stanley Products after thirty years. Ann Mast sold so many doll clothes Friday, she had to go home and sew more that night to have enough to sell on Saturday. Marek and Sarah Alimowski had great success with their colorful display of fresh strawberries. Others were selling soy candles, health products, sharks teeth necklaces, lovely handmade potholders, dish towels, and even baskets brought down from Holmes County, Ohio.

Sherry Gore, Pinecraft, Florida

Pennsylvania Dutch Ginger Cookies

1 cup butter or margarine
1 cup powdered sugar
1 tablespoon vinegar
2 teaspoons ground ginger

¾ teaspoon baking soda
¼ teaspoon salt
2¼ cups flour

Preheat oven to 400°. In large mixing bowl cream butter, sugar, and vinegar. Blend in remaining ingredients. Using floured rolling pin, roll dough to ⅛ inch thick on lightly floured surface. Cut into desired shapes. Place on ungreased cookie sheet. Bake 6 – 8 minutes or until light brown. Cool slightly; remove. Decorate with icing. Makes 3 – 4 dozen cookies.

Elizabeth (Bill and Ruth) Yoder, age 12

Ranger Cookies

1 cup shortening
1 cup brown sugar
1 cup sugar
2 beaten eggs
1 teaspoon vanilla
2 cups flour
½ teaspoon baking powder

1 teaspoon baking soda
½ teaspoon salt
2 cups oatmeal
3 cups crisp rice cereal
1 cup coconut flakes
1 cup nuts

Preheat oven to 350°. Cream together the shortening, brown sugar, and sugar. Add the beaten eggs and vanilla. In a separate bowl, combine the flour, baking powder, baking soda, and salt, and add that to the sugar and eggs mixture. Stir in oatmeal, rice cereal, coconut flakes, and nuts. Drop heaping spoonfuls onto greased cookie sheet. Bake 7 – 9 minutes. Makes 4 dozen large cookies.

Mary Miller, Zanesville, Ohio

Homemade Debbie Cookies

4 cups brown sugar
1½ cups butter
4 eggs
½ cup boiling water
4 teaspoons soda

2 cups flour
2 cups whole-wheat flour
2 teaspoons cinnamon
4 cups oatmeal

Filling

1 cup milk
5 tablespoons flour
1 cup shortening

1 teaspoon vanilla
½ teaspoon salt
¾ cup powdered sugar

Preheat oven to 325°. Cream sugar and butter; add eggs and mix well. Add soda to boiling water and add to mixture. Mix dry ingredients together and add. Mix well. Drop by tablespoonsful onto ungreased cookie sheet. Bake 10 – 12 minutes. Cool. *Filling:* Cook milk and flour together to form a thick paste. Cool. Cream rest of filling ingredients together and add flour mixture by spoonfuls. Spread filling on one cookie and top with another to form a sandwich cookie. Makes 6 dozen.

April Tinsley, Sarasota, Florida

Busy Day Cookies

½ cup shortening, softened
1 cup brown sugar
1 egg
¼ cup buttermilk or sour milk
½ teaspoon baking powder

½ teaspoon salt
1¾ cups flour
½ teaspoon soda
1 teaspoon vanilla
½ cup nuts

Preheat oven to 350°. Cream shortening, sugar, and egg. Add buttermilk and remaining ingredients. Mix well. Drop by teaspoonful onto cookie sheet. Bake 10 to 12 minutes.

Katie E. Graber, Arthur, Illinois

Can't Leave Alone Bars

So good you can't leave them alone!

1 box yellow cake mix
2 eggs
⅓ cup vegetable oil
½ cup butter

1 cup chocolate chips
1 (14 ounce) can sweetened
    condensed milk

Preheat oven to 350°. Combine cake mix, eggs, and oil in bowl. Set aside ¾ cup batter. Press batter into bottom of 13x9-inch pan. Melt butter, chocolate chips, and milk in a small saucepan. Pour over crust. Add remaining batter mixture by spooning dollops onto chocolate layer. Bake 35 – 40 minutes. Makes 24 bars.

Sherry Gore, Pinecraft, Florida

Mule Ear Cookies

1 cup shortening
1 cup brown sugar
1 cup sugar
2 eggs
½ cup molasses
4½ cups flour

4 teaspoons soda
4 teaspoons ginger
4 teaspoons cinnamon
2 teaspoons ground cloves
1 teaspoon salt

Cream shortening and sugars. Add eggs, molasses, and dry ingredients. Mix well and shape into logs. Refrigerate overnight. Preheat oven to 350°. Slice 1-inch thick and roll in sugar. Bake 10 – 12 minutes. Makes 5 – 6 dozen.

Ada Petersheim, longtime hostess at Der Dutchman
Restaurant, Pinecraft, Florida

[*The Pinecraft Pauper,* **December 16, 2010**]

Becky Fisher caught a burglar. As an eighty-one-year-old member of the Amish Church, Becky had seen a lot of activity in Pinecraft over the years. One day she put her detective instincts to work. While riding past her sister's unoccupied house in the village, Becky noticed a man inside the screened-in porch. A three-wheeler had been taken out of the shed. It was later determined the burglar broke a window and reached in and stole a set of keys setting nearby. Becky, thinking the fellow looked familiar, glanced up at him from her electric scooter and asked, "What's your name? Where do you live?" Incredibly he gave his name before fleeing on foot. Witnesses reported the incident to the police.

Sherry Gore, Pinecraft, Florida

Grandma's Oatmeal Raisin Cookies

1 cup shortening or margarine	1½ cups flour
1 cup brown sugar	1 teaspoon salt
1 cup white sugar	1 teaspoon soda
2 eggs	3 cups oatmeal
1 teaspoon vanilla	1 cup raisins

Preheat oven to 350°. Beat margarine and sugars together until fluffy. Add eggs and vanilla. Mix in dry ingredients and drop onto cookie sheets. Bake 8 minutes. For a special treat, I add ½ cup nuts, ½ cup coconut, and ½ cup butterscotch chips. Makes 4 dozen.

Mrs. Andrew (Ruth) Overholt, Pinecraft, Florida

16. Rebecca Fisher's Sauerkraut, *recipe page 101*

17. Macaroni and Cheese, *recipe page 113*

18. Grilled Lime Fish Fillets, *recipe page 152*

19. Pinecraft Winter Salad, *recipe page 79*

20. Chocolate Whoopie Pies, *recipe page 174*

21. Key Lime Pie, *recipe page 183*

23. Freezer Fruit-and-Yogurt Pops, *recipe page 231*

24. Final Exam Brownies, *recipe page 161*

25. Coconut Cream Pie, *recipe page 178*

26. Sunburst Lemon Bars, *recipe page 167*

27. Dark-Chocolate-Covered Caramels with Sea Salt, *recipe page 229*

28. Orange Pie, *recipe page 184*

29. Sand Dollar Sugar Cookies, *recipe page 163*

30. Carrot Cake, *recipe page 191*

31. Dutch Blueberry Babies, *recipe page 51*

No-Bake Cookies

¼ cup butter

½ cup milk

2 cups sugar

4 tablespoons cocoa

2 tablespoons peanut butter

3 cups quick oats

Heat first four ingredients until butter is melted. Boil 3 minutes, then remove from heat and add peanut butter and oats. Drop by spoonfuls on wax paper. Makes 4 dozen.

April Tinsley, Sarasota, Florida

Final Exam Brownies

Kathleen (David) Schlabach of Sunnyside Mennonite Church and Rachelle (James) Graber of Hope Mennonite Church graduated from Sunnyside Mennonite School May 25, 2009. The graduates started school the day of the September 11, 2001, terrorist attacks.

4 oz. unsweetened chocolate, chopped

1 cup butter

1 cup sugar

4 eggs

1 teaspoonful vanilla

1 cup flour

2 cups miniature marshmallows

1 cup chopped pecans or walnuts, optional

1½ cups semisweet chocolate chips

Preheat oven to 350°. Melt chocolate and butter; stir until smooth. Cool. Add sugar, eggs, and vanilla and beat until smooth. Add flour and mix well. Fold in marshmallows, nuts, and ½ cup chocolate chips. Pour into a greased 13x9-inch pan and sprinkle with 1 cup chocolate chips. Bake 30 minutes or until top is set. Do not overbake. (See color plate 24 for illustration.)

Sherry Gore, Pinecraft, Florida

Golatschen Christmas Cookies

Golatschen is the German word for "Pastry."

⅔ cup sugar
1 cup butter, softened
½ teaspoon almond extract

2 cups flour
any flavor jelly

Icing

1 cup powdered sugar
2 – 3 teaspoons water

1½ teaspoons almond extract

Preheat oven to 350°. Cream sugar, butter, and extract. Add flour and mix well. Shape into 1-inch balls and place on cookie sheets. Press thumb in centers and fill with 1 teaspoon jelly. Bake 10 – 12 minutes. Mix icing ingredients, adding more water until icing is runny. Drizzle over warm cookies.

Sherry Gore, Pinecraft, Florida

Ginger Snap Cookies

1½ cups sugar
1 cup butter
2 eggs
½ cup molasses
3¾ cups flour

¾ teaspoon cinnamon
¼ teaspoon ground cloves
¼ teaspoon ginger
2½ teaspoons soda
¾ teaspoon salt

Cream sugar, butter, eggs, and molasses together. Add rest of ingredients and form into small balls. Roll in sugar before baking at 300°.

Mrs. Dan (Martha) Stutzman, Sarasota, Florida

Monster Cookies

¾ cup butter, melted
1 cup sugar
1 cup brown sugar
4 eggs, beaten
1¾ cups creamy peanut butter

4 cups quick oatmeal
2½ tablespoons flour
2½ teaspoons baking soda
2 cups chocolate chips
1 cup M&M's

Preheat oven to 350°. Mix first five ingredients. Gradually add soda, then stir in rest of ingredients. Let set 20 minutes, then shape cookies and roll in powdered sugar. Bake 12 minutes. Do not overbake.

Mrs. Sam (Martha) Hostetler, Pinecraft, Florida

Sand Dollar Sugar Cookies

3 cups brown sugar
½ pound shortening
3 eggs
1 tablespoon vanilla

½ tablespoon cream of tartar
2 pounds flour
½ tablespoon soda
2 cups buttermilk

Preheat oven to 350°. Cream sugar and shortening. Add eggs and vanilla. Mix cream of tartar and flour, and dissolve soda in milk. Add mixtures alternately to the sugar mixture. Roll out and cut with round cookie cutter. Bake 15 – 20 minutes. Decorate with white royal frosting to look like sand dollars by piping a border and five teardrops. Let harden. "Flood" rest of cookie top with frosting. Take care not to fill in teardrops. (See color plate 29 for illustration.)

Sherry Gore, Pinecraft, Florida

Royal Frosting

4 cups powdered sugar
6 tablespoons warm water

2½ tablespoons meringue powder

Whip until perfectly smooth and creamy, about 1 minute.

Sherry Gore, Pinecraft, Florida

Date Balls

2 eggs
½ cup butter or margarine
1 cup sugar
1 package dates, chopped

2 cups crisp rice cereal
1 cup chopped nuts
coconut

Beat eggs in saucepan. Add butter and sugar, and melt over medium heat, stirring constantly. Add dates and cook over low heat. Remove from heat when mixture is clear. Add rice cereal and nuts. Shape into balls, roll in coconut, and cool. Makes 3 dozen.

Treva Slabaugh, Pinecraft, Florida

Outrageous Chocolate Chip Cookies

1 cup sugar
⅔ cup brown sugar
1 cup butter or margarine
1 cup peanut butter
1 teaspoon vanilla
2 eggs

2 cups flour
2 teaspoons soda
1 teaspoon baking powder
½ teaspoon salt
1½ cups quick oats
1½ cups chocolate chips

Preheat oven to 350°. Combine sugars, butter, and peanut butter until creamy and well-blended. Add vanilla and eggs and beat well. In a small mixing bowl, mix flour, soda, baking powder, and salt. Add to creamed mixture, then stir in oats and chocolate chips and mix well. Drop by tablespoonsful onto ungreased cookie sheet. Bake 10 – 12 minutes or until golden brown.

Mrs. David (Lillian) Yoder, Hicksville, Ohio

December 28, 2009
Sunnyside Amish Mennonite Church, Sarasota, Florida

With downpours on and off on Christmas Day, many wondered aloud if the annual Pinecraft Christmas Parade would be canceled. Just in the nick of time, the rain disappeared and the sun came out, as did about a thousand folks to enjoy the festivities. Our very own hometown "Hokey Parade," as one fellow called it, included tractors, a boy on a unicycle, a boat, some sort of smallish flying machine, a swamp buggy, a horse and buggy, lots of rollerbladers, children on scooters, a monster truck, and some brave folks riding in a goat-pulled cart. David R. Miller was familiar to most, but the goat was nobody we knew.

If you're wondering what the story is on the brand-new yellow boxes placed in Pinecraft, you only have to pay one dollar to find out. The distribution boxes are for the new publication *The Pinecraft Pauper*, Pinecraft's village newspaper. The box has a slot for your dollar bill, but the paper is sold on the honor system. One box is located at the Pinecraft Post Office, and the other is at Yoder's Restaurant, next to the *USA Today*. The *Pauper* is better.

According to publisher Leon Hostetler, *The Pinecraft Pauper* has a mishmash of interesting content, with articles ranging from human interest and local events to articles about interesting birds. Also included are recipes, poems, and puzzles. Daniel Fisher, who fashioned the distinctive boxes by hand, serves as editor.

Sherry Gore, Pinecraft, Florida

A recent phone call from a friend in Pennsylvania: "So when did you start writing for the **Popcorn Popper?***" I'm sure she meant* **The Pinecraft Pauper.**

Mast Cookies

1 cup butter
1 cup sour cream
2 cups brown sugar
2 teaspoons soda

2 eggs
5 cups flour (approximate)
½ teaspoon vanilla

Frosting

3 – 4 cups powdered sugar
¼ cup milk

½ cup butter

Preheat oven to 350°. Mix all cookie ingredients. Roll out and cut dough. Bake 10 minutes. Mix frosting ingredients and top cookies with frosting.

Annie (Mast) Graber, former owner of Dutch Oven Restaurant, Sarasota, Florida

Powder Snowballs

2 cups flour, sifted
¾ teaspoon salt
1 cup unsalted butter
½ cup sugar

1 tablespoon vanilla
1 cup finely chopped pecans
¾ cup powdered sugar

Preheat oven to 325°. Grease two cookie sheets. Sift flour and salt over a piece of wax paper. In a medium-size bowl, cream butter and sugar until fluffy. Add vanilla and stir. Stir in flour mixture and add pecans. After dusting hands with powdered sugar, form dough into 1-inch balls. Bake 25 minutes or until light brown. Cool 15 – 20 minutes, then roll in powdered sugar. Makes 3 dozen.

Sherry Gore, Pinecraft, Florida

Sunburst Lemon Bars

2 cups flour

½ cup powdered sugar

1 cup butter

Filling

4 eggs, slightly beaten

1 teaspoon baking powder

2 cups sugar

¼ cup flour

¼ cup lemon juice

Glaze

1 cup powdered sugar

2 – 3 tablespoons lemon juice

Preheat oven to 350°. Mix flour, powdered sugar, and butter until crumbly. Press evenly into the bottom of an ungreased 13x9-inch pan. Bake 20 – 30 minutes or until golden brown. In a large bowl, combine all filling ingredients except lemon juice. Blend well and stir in lemon juice. Pour filling over warm base and bake an additional 25 – 30 minutes. Set aside to cool. Combine glaze ingredients, using enough lemon juice to reach desired consistency. Blend until smooth. I sometimes add a little lemon rind for more flavor. Glaze cooled bars. Makes 18 bars. (See color plate 26 for illustration.)

Mrs. Nelson (Dorothy) Martin, Martinsburg, Pennsylvania

Butterscotch Nut Bars

1 package yellow cake mix

1½ cups chopped pecans

¾ cup butter, melted

2 (8 ounce) packages cream cheese

1 cup brown sugar

Preheat oven to 350°. Combine cake mix, pecans, and butter. Press into 13x9-inch pan. Mix cream cheese and brown sugar together and spread on top of crust mix. Bake until golden brown.

Irene Miller, Pinecraft, Florida

Chewy Granola Bars

2½ cups oatmeal
4¾ cups crispy rice cereal
¾ cup raisins or pecans
½ cup coconut
½ cup graham cracker crumbs
2 tablespoons butter

¾ pound marshmallows
⅛ cup peanut butter
¼ cup honey
2 tablespoons vegetable oil
½ cup mini chocolate chips

Mix oatmeal, crispy rice cereal, raisins, coconut, and cracker crumbs together. Mix butter, marshmallows, peanut butter, honey, and vegetable oil and stir into cereal mixture. Stir in chocolate chips and press into two 13x9-inch pans. Makes 3 dozen.

Sherry Gore, Pinecraft, Florida

Caramel Bars

32 caramels
1 (14 ounce) can sweetened
 condensed milk
1 cup quick oats
1 cup flour

¾ cup butter
¾ cup brown sugar
1 teaspoon baking soda
1 cup milk chocolate chips

Preheat oven to 350°. Melt caramels and milk in microwave until melted and smooth. Mix oats, flour, butter, brown sugar, and baking soda like pie dough. Put a little over ½ of crumb mixture in 13x9-inch pan. Bake 10 minutes. Sprinkle with chocolate chips and spread caramel mixture over top. Top with remaining crumbs and bake no longer than 12 – 15 minutes.

Emily Kennell, Pinecraft, Florida

Salty Crispy Bars

1 package yellow cake mix	⅓ cup butter, softened
1 egg	3 cups mini marshmallows

Topping

⅔ cup corn syrup	12 ounces peanut butter chips
¼ cup butter or margarine	2 cups crispy rice cereal
2 teaspoons vanilla	2 cups salty peanuts

Preheat oven to 350°. In a large bowl, combine cake mix, egg, and butter, mixing until crumbly. Press into ungreased 13x9-inch pan. Bake 15 minutes or until golden brown. Remove and cover entire crust with marshmallows. Return to oven just long enough for marshmallows to start to puff. Cool while preparing topping. In a large saucepan heat corn syrup, butter or margarine, vanilla, and chips until melted and smooth, stirring constantly. Remove from heat; stir in cereal and nuts. Spread topping over marshmallows. Chill; cut into bars.

Shannon Torkelson, Alberta, Canada

A beloved grandmother passed away leaving a legacy of 262 grandchildren and great-grandchildren. Mrs. Homer (Martha Mullet) Gingerich (also lovingly known as "the Gingerich Grandma") went into eternity on May 30, 2010. She was a member of Palm Grove Mennonite Church. At age ninety-four, Martha was the epitome of a devoted grandmother, for each grandchild who spoke at her funeral service claimed, "I was Grandma's favorite."

Hello Dolly Apple Bars

4 cups diced apples (Granny Smith are best for this recipe)
1½ cups sugar
½ cup oil
3 eggs
2 cups flour

2 teaspoons baking soda
1½ teaspoons cinnamon
1 teaspoon salt
½ cup chopped nuts
½ cup raisins
1 cup chocolate chips

Preheat oven to 350°. Mix all ingredients together and spread into 13x9-inch pan. Bake 35–40 minutes. Makes 18 bars.

Mrs. Homer (Martha) Gingerich, Pinecraft, Florida

Pumpkin Bars

¾ cup margarine
2 cups sugar
2 cups pumpkin
4 eggs
2 cups flour
2 teaspoons baking powder

1 teaspoon cinnamon
½ teaspoon soda
½ teaspoon salt
¼ teaspoon nutmeg
1 cup chopped nuts

Frosting

3 ounces cream cheese
⅓ cup margarine

3 cups powdered sugar
1 teaspoon vanilla

Preheat oven to 350°. Cream margarine and sugar together. Add pumpkin and eggs. Add remaining ingredients. Spread into a greased 10½x15½-inch jelly-roll pan. Bake 30–35 minutes. Cool, mix frosting ingredients, and frost.

Sarah Joy Beiler, Pinecraft, Florida

Pecan Pie Bars

Crust

3 cups flour

1 cup margarine

½ cup sugar

½ teaspoon salt

Filling

2 tablespoons flour

1½ cups sugar

4 eggs

1½ cups light corn syrup

1½ teaspoons vanilla

2 cups chopped pecans

3 tablespoons margarine, melted

Preheat oven to 350°. Grease bottom and sides of 10x15-inch cookie sheet. Prepare crust in a large bowl. Mix until it resembles coarse crumbs; press firmly into pan and bake 20 minutes. Meanwhile, prepare filling. Mix flour and sugar. Add slightly beaten eggs, corn syrup, vanilla, nuts, and margarine. Spread evenly over crust and bake 25 – 30 minutes longer. Cool and cut into bars.

Mrs. Andrew (Ruth) Overholt, Pinecraft, Florida

Mud Hen Bars

Make these once and you'll have a family favorite!

½ cup shortening

1 cup white sugar

1 egg

2 egg yolks

1 teaspoon baking powder

1½ cups flour

¼ teaspoon salt

1 cup nuts

½ cup chocolate chips

1 cup mini marshmallows

2 egg whites

1 cup brown sugar

Preheat oven to 350°. Mix first seven ingredients (through salt) and press into 13x9-inch pan. Sprinkle with nuts, chocolate chips, and marshmallows. Beat egg whites until stiff; fold in brown sugar. Spread on top. Bake 30 – 40 minutes. Makes 18 bars.

Mrs. Sylvanus (Mary) Hershberger, Millersburg, Ohio

Chocolate Fudgy Crinkles

1½ cups (about 9 ounces) bittersweet chocolate chips, divided

3 large egg whites, room temperature

¼ teaspoon cream of tartar

2½ cups powdered sugar, divided

½ cup unsweetened cocoa powder

1 tablespoon cornstarch

¼ teaspoon salt

Preheat oven to 350°. Spray 2 large baking sheets with nonstick cooking spray. Melt 1 cup chocolate chips in double boiler. Cool slightly. Beat egg whites and cream of tartar in large bowl to soft peaks. Gradually beat in 1 cup powdered sugar. Continue beating until mixture resembles soft marshmallow crème. Whisk 1 cup powdered sugar, cocoa, cornstarch, and salt in medium bowl and blend. Beat dry ingredients into meringue. Stir in melted chocolate and ½ cup chocolate chips. Place remaining ½ cup sugar in bowl. Roll 1 rounded tablespoon dough into ball; roll in sugar, coating thickly. Place on prepared sheet. Repeat with remaining dough, spacing 2 inches apart. Bake until puffed and tops crack, about 10 minutes. Let set on baking sheet about 5 minutes before removing. Place on cooling rack. Makes 18 cookies.

Sherry Gore, Pinecraft, Florida

Grape Jelly Bars

2 cups quick oats

2½ cups flour

1 cup oil

1 egg, beaten

1 teaspoon vanilla

1½ cups sugar

½ cup brown sugar

½ teaspoon salt

1 teaspoon baking powder

2 cups jelly

Preheat oven to 350°. Mix all ingredients except jelly and press half of mixture into 13x9-inch pan. Spread jelly on top and top with rest of crumbs. Bake 30 minutes. Makes 18 bars.

Anna Musser, Manheim, Pennsylvania

Coffee Bars

2⅔ cups brown sugar
1 cup oil
2 eggs
1 teaspoon baking soda
1 teaspoon salt

3 cups flour
1 cup coffee, room temperature
12 ounces chocolate chips
1 cup walnuts or pecans

Preheat oven at 350°. Combine sugar, oil, and eggs in large mixing bowl. Add dry ingredients, alternating with coffee. Spread on jelly roll pan. Top with chocolate chips and desired nuts. Bake 30 minutes. Makes 18 – 24 bars.

Sherry Gore, Pinecraft, Florida

Peanut Butter Squares

½ cup sugar
½ cup brown sugar
½ cup butter
⅓ cup peanut butter
1 egg

1 cup flour
1 cup quick oats
½ teaspoon soda
¼ teaspoon salt

Peanut Butter Frosting

1½ cups powdered sugar
¼ cup peanut butter

3 tablespoons milk, divided
3 tablespoons cocoa

Cream sugars, butter, and peanut butter. Then add remaining ingredients. Bake in greased jelly roll pan. Combine powdered sugar, peanut butter, and 2 tablespoons milk. Set aside ⅓ cup of this mixture. Spread remaining mixture on bars. Beat remaining milk and cocoa into reserved mixture, and spread on top. Cut into squares. Makes 24 bars.

Mrs. John Troyer, Pinecraft, Florida

I don't believe I ever brought home a leftover whoopie pie when Esther and I sold our baked goods at Yoder's Farmers' Market in Pinecraft. They usually sold out in the morning. Minister Jason Gingerich, when working at the Bulk-N-Natural store, would walk over each Saturday and purchase two chocolate whoopie pies for breakfast. We sold them for 50 cents. Some English call them BFOs (big fat Oreos) or gobs, but the Amish call them whoopie pies. An old story says Amish whoopie pies were made of leftover cake batter and packed in children's lunch boxes. When they opened the box at school and found the treat, they'd shout, "Whoopie!"

Sherry Gore, Pinecraft, Florida

Chocolate Whoopie Pies

1½ cups shortening
3 cups sugar
3 egg yolks, beaten
3 teaspoons vanilla
1½ cups buttermilk
(or sour milk)

3 teaspoons baking soda
2 teaspoons salt
1½ cups hot water
1½ cups cocoa
6 cups flour

Preheat oven at 350°. Cream together shortening and sugar. Add egg yolks and vanilla. Stir in buttermilk. Add baking soda, salt, hot water, cocoa, and flour. Beat well. Drop by tablespoon onto greased cookie sheet and bake 12 minutes. Makes approximately 40 whoopie pies.

Sherry Gore, Pinecraft, Florida

Filling

1½ cups white shortening
(not butter flavored)
5 tablespoons milk

3 cups powdered sugar
3 teaspoons vanilla
3 egg whites, beaten stiff

Cream shortening and milk. Add powdered sugar and vanilla; mix well. Beat in egg whites until filling is fluffy.

To assemble pies, spread a heaping spoonful of filling on flat side of half the cookies. Top with remaining cookies. (See color plate 20 for illustration.)

Lisa Miller, Chouteau, Oklahoma

Young Sterling, one of the two newborn baby raccoons we have been bottle feeding, didn't make it, but "Daniel Boone" looks fat and happy! Nathan Overholt found them in Ben Smoker's attic in Pinecraft. Katie Troyer said, "Ha, a Pinecraft raccoon. They have fat genes. I have never seen such big coons out in the wild as there are here in Pinecraft."

Pies

Custard Pie

4 ounces cream cheese	pinch of salt
¾ cup sugar	1 teaspoon vanilla
4 eggs	1 unbaked pie shell
2 cups milk	nutmeg
½ cup sweetened condensed milk	

Preheat oven to 400°. Beat softened cream cheese and sugar together. Add eggs one at a time and beat well after each addition. Heat milk and add to mixture. Add condensed milk, salt, and vanilla. Beat until very foamy and pour into unbaked pie shell. Sprinkle with nutmeg. Bake 10 minutes; reduce heat to 350° and bake 25 minutes more or until done.

Mrs. Andrew (Ruth) Overholt, Pinecraft, Florida

Coconut Cream Pie

2½ cups milk	1 baked pie shell
1 cup sugar	3 egg whites
¼ cup cornstarch	1 teaspoon cream of tartar
dash of salt	1 teaspoon coconut flavoring
¾ cup fresh or sweetened coconut flakes	½ cup sugar
	extra coconut flakes

Bring 2 cups milk to a boil. Mix sugar, cornstarch, and salt together. Stir into hot milk. Bring to a boil, stirring constantly. Remove from heat and cool. Add coconut and pour into baked crust. Top with meringue.

To prepare meringue, beat together egg whites, cream of tartar, and coconut flavoring, until stiff. Gradually beat in sugar. Spread on pie. Sprinkle coconut on top of meringue. Bake at 400° for 20 minutes or until golden brown. (See color plate 25 for illustration.)

Fannie Kay Yoder, Chouteau, Oklahoma

Shoofly Pie

1 cup flour	¾ cup hot water
⅔ cup brown sugar	1 cup cane molasses
1 tablespoon butter	1 egg
1 teaspoon soda	1 unbaked pie shell

Preheat oven to 400°. Mix flour, brown sugar, and butter with a fork until crumbly. Measure out half of crumbs and set aside. Dissolve soda in water. Add molasses and egg, then stir into half of the crumbs. Pour into an unbaked pie shell and top with remaining crumbs. Bake 10 minutes, then reduce heat to 325° and bake an additional 30 minutes.

Susan (Miller) Hershberger

Fudge Swirl Toffee Pie

½ cup semisweet chocolate chips
2 tablespoons milk
1 (8 ounce) package cream cheese
1 (7 ounce) jar marshmallow
　　crème

½ cup brown sugar
1 cup chopped almonds, toasted
1 (8 ounce) container nondairy
　　whipped topping
1 chocolate wafer pie crust

Melt chips with milk and set aside. Combine cream cheese, marshmallow crème, and sugar; mix well until blended. Fold in the almonds and half of nondairy whipped topping. Spread half of marshmallow mixture into pie crust. Cover with chocolate mixture and swirl through the layers with a knife. Keep in refrigerator. Cut into 6 – 8 servings and enjoy. You can also use a regular pie crust.

Emily Kennell, Pinecraft, Florida

Yoder's Restaurant
[from *The Pinecraft Pauper* (ed. 7)]

　　Mary Fisher and I were waiting in line for lunch and overheard two fellows say they drove down from Tallahassee especially to eat at Yoder's, having seen it featured on the cable TV program *Man v. Food*. Yoder's was voted #68 on America's top 101 best places to chow down. Mary started off with a chilled pea salad. She was kind enough to offer some to me. With the first bite, I left Yoder's. I'm sure of it. You see, with each taste I felt as though I were sitting on a white, wrap-around porch in Georgia on a hot summer day, relishing the coolness of the petite early peas. Mary said I never left — that I was sitting there the whole time. But I beg to differ.

　　"I'll have the Reuben sandwich," she told Cory, our server. The sandwich came stuffed with "so much corned beef, it's coming out the side," she proclaimed. "My sandwich is so wide it won't fit in my mouth." Mary's entrée came with a little cup of Thousand Island dressing to be used as a dipping sauce.

When I asked Mary what kind of cheese her Reuben was made with, she smiled and said, "Delicious cheese." Their bread was grilled perfectly and slathered with Swiss. Mary saved half to take home to her husband, John.

Lucky John.

We couldn't help but notice the two folks sitting at the table next to us. They had platters of turkey breast on their table. You'd have thought it was Thanksgiving Day. But it wasn't. It was Wednesday.

I ordered the crab cake sandwich with a side of French fries. My meal came with a salad-sized serving of lettuce and tomato. Yoder's doesn't skimp on condiments. Cory delivered tartar sauce, cocktail sauce, and ketchup to my side of the table. The sandwich, which came on a soft Kaiser roll, was too big to hold all at once, so I cut it in half. I discreetly pushed the roll down a bit, for like Mary's sandwich, mine was also too wide for my mouth. The crab cake was deep-fried golden brown crisp and tasted like something you'd expect to get at a beachfront eatery. It was delicious; something I will definitely order again.

Mary and I are proficient talkers, but there was an occasional lull in our conversation for sounds of *mmm, mmm.*

We delighted in our time together and couldn't help but notice there was a constant stream of pie going by. Almost a pie parade, if you will. Even with more than twenty-five varieties to choose from, I don't think there's a pie there I haven't tried. We settled on a strawberry pie taster to split. We were full, but a visit to Yoder's isn't complete without dessert.

The overflowing dish of pie came on a doily-lined plate. Sweet. As I ate my half of the pie, Mary looked at me incredulously and said, "Sherry Gore, your eyes are twinkling."

Yoder's Restaurant is open from 6:00 a.m. to 8:00 p.m. Monday through Saturday for dining in or carry-out.

Raisin Cream Pie

2 cups raisins
4 cups water
1 cup brown sugar
1 cup sugar
2 tablespoons flour
2 tablespoons cornstarch

4 egg yolks
1 teaspoon salt
1 cup milk or half-and-half
1 teaspoon vanilla
1 baked pie shell
nondairy whipped topping

Combine raisins, water, and brown sugar in a saucepan. Bring to a boil; turn off heat and let soak a few hours or overnight. Bring back to a boil and add sugar. Mix flour, cornstarch, egg yolks, salt, and milk, and slowly add to raisins to thicken. Add vanilla last. Pour into baked pie shell and top with nondairy whipped topping. Makes 1 10-inch deep-dish pie.

Mrs. Ralph (Sarah) Schlabach

Peanut Butter Pie

1 small box vanilla instant
   pudding
1¾ cups milk
4 ounces cream cheese, softened

⅓ of (8 ounce) tub of nondairy
   whipped topping
¼ cup peanut butter
⅔ cup powdered sugar
1 baked pie crust

Mix instant pudding with milk according to directions on box. After pudding sets, beat in softened cream cheese and ⅓ tub of whipped topping. In a separate bowl, blend peanut butter and powdered sugar until crumbly. When crust is cool, spread ⅔ cup peanut butter crumbles on bottom of crust. Fill with pudding mixture and top with remaining nondairy whipped topping. Garnish with remaining peanut butter crumbs.

Sarah McGuire, Montgomery, Iowa

Pumpkin Pie

2 eggs, separated
¾ cup brown sugar
1 cup pumpkin
1 tablespoon flour, heaping

1 teaspoon pumpkin pie spice
1½ cups half-and-half
1 unbaked pie shell

Preheat oven to 425°. Beat egg yolks, brown sugar, pumpkin, flour, and spice well. Add half-and-half. Beat egg whites and add last. Pour into unbaked pie shell. Bake 15 minutes; reduce heat to 350° and bake 30 minutes longer.

Susan (Miller) Hershberger

Lemon Sour Cream Pie

1 cup sugar
¼ cup cornstarch
⅛ teaspoon salt
1 cup milk (more if needed)
3 egg yolks

¼ cup butter
¼ cup fresh lemon juice (or more)
1 cup sour cream
1 tablespoon grated lemon peel
1 baked pie shell

Combine and cook first five ingredients 2 minutes. Add rest of ingredients and pour into a baked pie shell. Serve with your favorite topping.

Ada Miller, Millersburg, Ohio

Dutch Apple Pie

4 cups sliced apples
¾ cup sugar
½ teaspoon cinnamon

2 tablespoons butter, melted
1 unbaked pie shell

Topping

¾ cup flour
⅓ cup brown sugar

½ teaspoon cinnamon
⅓ cup butter

Mix apples, sugar, cinnamon, and butter, and put in pie shell. Mix topping ingredients and sprinkle on top. Bake at 375° until apples are done.

Laura Yoder, Sarasota, Florida

Key Lime Pie

½ cup fresh lime juice
1 (14 ounce) can sweetened
   condensed milk
1½ – 2 cups nondairy whipped
   topping

green food coloring (optional)
1 baked pie crust
additional whipped topping

Beat lime juice and milk together. Add whipped topping and food coloring, and pour into pie crust. Top with nondairy whipped topping. Fresh lemon juice will work same as lime. (See color plate 21 for illustration.)

Laura Yoder, Sarasota, Florida

October 1, 2000
Sunnyside Amish Mennonite Church, Sarasota, Florida

Mary and I were seated in the dining room by the window. This was especially nice as this particular morning was the kick-off for Pinecraft Days. The sidewalks were bustling with snowbirds from communities across the country. Jackie was our waitress.

Mom's now offers breakfast, lunch, and dinner, buffet style. The breakfast buffet was a mere $5.95. With so many home-cooked dishes to choose from, I thought to limit my portions so I could try a little bit of everything. No matter how hard I tried, it just wasn't possible. There was fried corn mush and a rich, creamy tomato gravy to go on top, Belgian-style waffles, feather-light pancakes, sausage patties, bacon, homemade Danish pastry covered in frosting, southern grits, and sausage gravy and biscuits. Too much for anyone to sample even just a bite of each.

The only thing missing was the scrapple.

One of the egg dishes reminded me of a Denver scramble. It was made with tasty, bite-sized chunky potatoes and diced bell peppers. I poured a small ladleful of cheese sauce and a spoonful of golden sautéed mushrooms and onions over the top and had a gourmet dish.

The cooks, Jim Janda and Katherine Schrock, must fire up the kitchen stoves at dawn. The home fries we ate were lightly salted and crisp on both sides. It was as though the cook lovingly fried each one individually and delivered them straight from the skillet onto my plate — I'm especially fond of potatoes, and this was the best potato dish I can remember eating. Mary proclaimed them "lovely."

Sarah Beiler was prepping the buffet for the lunch crowd, setting out little dishes of puddings. Only the sign posted nearby betrayed they were sugar-free; they looked scrumptious. There were also generous servings of blueberry delight awaiting the lunch crowd. Before leaving our table, Mary insisted we order one chocolate crinkle cookie to share — just so I could try one. "You've never had anything like these." So I ordered two. She was right. They looked like dark chocolate cookies coated with a light dusting of powdered sugar, but they tasted more like a dreamy, rich fudge you would expect at Christmastime. I would trade $600 for one right now, but Mom's only charged me 65 cents on Thursday.

Sherry Gore, Pinecraft, Florida

Orange Pie

2 cups sugar, divided
1 tablespoon cornstarch
    or Clear Jel
1½ cups water
1 tablespoon orange Jell-O
    or Kool-Aid

juice of 2 – 3 oranges
1 (3 ounce) package cream
    cheese, softened
4 cups (12 ounces) nondairy
    whipped topping, divided
1 baked pie shell

Cook 1 cup sugar, cornstarch, and water until clear and thickened. Add Jell-O and cool. Juice oranges and add to sugar mixture. Beat cream cheese, remaining sugar, and 2 cups nondairy whipped topping until fluffy. Spread into bottom of baked pie shell and pour orange mixture on top. Top with additional whipped topping and enjoy. (See color plate 28 for illustration.)

Arlene Mast, Pinecraft, Florida

Pecan Pie

3 eggs	1 teaspoon vanilla
½ cup brown sugar	⅛ teaspoon salt
¾ cup light corn syrup	½ cup chopped pecans
¼ cup water	3 tablespoons butter, melted

Preheat oven to 350°. Place first six ingredients (through salt) in blender and mix well. Place pecans in pie crust; add mixture and melted butter. Bake 10 minutes; reduce heat to 325° and bake 30 minutes longer.

Sadie A. Beachy, Pinecraft, Florida

Bob Andy Pie

What is a Bob Andy pie? As the story is told, an Amish farmer came in from working in the fields, took one bite of this delicious pie, and said, "This pie is as good as Bob and Andy" (which were his two prize gelding work horses).

2 tablespoons flour	¼ cup butter
½ teaspoon cream of tartar	3 eggs
1 teaspoon cinnamon	3 cups milk
2 cups brown sugar	2 unbaked pie shells

Preheat oven to 400°. Combine dry ingredients. Add butter and eggs. Mix well. Stir in milk. Pour into unbaked pie crusts and bake until firm, about 45 minutes. Makes two 9-inch pies.

Mrs. Sylvanus (Mary) Hershberger, Millersburg, Ohio

Amish Vanilla Crumb Pie

½ cup brown sugar

1 tablespoon flour

¼ cup dark corn syrup

1½ teaspoons vanilla

1 egg, beaten

1 cup water

1 unbaked pie shell

Crumbs

1 cup flour

½ teaspoon soda

½ cup brown sugar

⅛ teaspoon salt

½ teaspoon cream of tartar

¼ cup butter

Preheat oven to 350°. Combine brown sugar, flour, corn syrup, vanilla, and egg in a 2-quart saucepan. Slowly stir in water and cook over medium heat, stirring until mixture starts to boil. Let cool. Mix crumb ingredients until crumbly. Pour cooled pie mixture into pie shell and top with crumbs. Bake 40 minutes or until golden brown.

Laura Yoder, Sarasota, Florida

CARING FOR YOUR ROLLING PIN

A wooden rolling pin can last a lifetime. To ensure years of service, hand wash it quickly in hot soapy water and dry it completely with a towel. Avoid putting it in a dishwasher, as soaking for too long will shorten the life of your rolling pin.

For heavenly pies, a heavy pan with a dark finish is best for baking. It will absorb more heat and brown more deeply than a pan with a shiny, reflective metal surface.

TIP

The second day of a diet is always easier than the first.
By the second day, you're off it.

Pineapple Pie

1 large (20 ounce) can crushed
    pineapple with juice
2 small boxes vanilla instant
    pudding
1 (16 ounce) container sour cream

graham cracker pie crust
nondairy whipped topping
    for garnish
maraschino cherry halves
    for garnish

Stir pineapple and pudding together. Fold in sour cream and spread in crust. Top with nondairy whipped topping and cherry halves.

Sherry Gore, Pinecraft, Florida

Angel Cream Pie

2 cups heavy cream
½ cup sugar
3 tablespoons flour
⅛ teaspoon salt

1 teaspoon vanilla
2 egg whites
1 unbaked pie shell

Preheat oven to 350°. Heat cream (do not boil). Stir together dry ingredients and slowly add hot cream while stirring. Add vanilla. Beat egg whites until stiff and fold into cream mixture. Pour into unbaked pie shell. Bake 25 minutes, just until cream sets in center.

Coleen (Witmer) Swartzentruber

Pie Crust

3 cups flour
1 teaspoon salt
1 tablespoon sugar
1 cup butter-flavored Crisco

¼ cup milk
¼ cup water
¼ cup oil

Mix flour, salt, sugar, and Crisco until crumbly. Combine remaining ingredients and add to crumbs. Stir only enough to make a dough; do not knead. Makes a 9-inch double crust or three thin crusts.

Edith Good, Wooster, Ohio

But You All Look Alike!

Considering the Amish and Mennonite snowbirds in Pinecraft come from many different orders throughout the country, there are few subtle differences recognizable to the untrained eye. When asked by a tourist, "How do you know where someone is from?" one Mennonite girl simply explained, "By their coverings ye shall know them."

February 27, 2008
Sunnyside Amish Mennonite Church, Sarasota, Florida

Thursday afternoon brought hundreds of folks to our place here in Pinecraft. No, not for a visit, but for the auction of Gary Eash's estate, where he lived on Graber Avenue. Neighbor Henry Detweiler, who held the sale, said, "Had I known there would be such a turnout, I'd have made a pot of my cowboy stew." The auction started the same time the famous Pioneer Trails bus pulled in, so that crowd came over to check out the doings on this side of Bahia Vista Street. Several folks were glad for the coffee and Fannie Kay Yoder's chocolate cream pie.

The first ever Sunnyside School banquet fund-raiser was held Friday evening with quite a turnout. Minister-teacher Jason Gingerich and his wife, Angie, pulled out all the stops, making it an event to remember. I missed out on meeting the Virginia Beach fellow responsible for grilling pork, chicken, and potatoes, Alvin Zook.

Sherry Gore, Pinecraft, Florida

Fannie Kay's Chocolate Cream Pie

This pie tastes like a chocolate explosion in your mouth!

2½ cups milk	dash of salt
1 cup sugar	½ teaspoon vanilla
¼ cup cocoa	1 baked pie shell
¼ cup cornstarch	nondairy whipped topping

Bring 2 cups of milk to a boil. In separate bowl, mix sugar, cocoa, and cornstarch together. Stir in ½ cup of milk. Stir into hot milk. Bring to boil, stirring constantly. Add salt and vanilla. Remove from heat and cool. Pour into baked crust and top with whipped topping.

Mrs. Mervin (Fannie Kay) Yoder, Chouteau, Oklahoma

Who is it that churns out the goodies from the bakery at Yoder's Restaurant? It is Mary Yoder and staff. Mrs. Yoder's outlook for the winter is this: "We're gonna have an awesome season. Bring it on!"

Baking gives her pleasure, she declared, for she is "carrying on Mom's tradition." I offered her a million dollars for the secret pie dough recipe, but she said it would take more than that. It crushed me right down, for a million was all I had on me.

Daniel Fisher, editor, *The Pinecraft Pauper*

The trouble with a marriage often starts when a man spends so much time earning his salt that he forgets his sugar.

August 27, 2008
Sunnyside Amish Mennonite Church, Sarasota, Florida

"It's all about pies!" That's the motto at Yoder's Restaurant as they celebrate their thirty-third birthday. Pie tasters are on the menu this month, and every thirty-third customer receives a free whole pie. That's quite a free gift. I mastered the technique of making pie at Yoder's two years ago during the Christmas holiday. Seven of us rolled out 1,700 pie crusts in one day. I went to bed that night with sore muscles and an unforgettable lesson learned: Pie making is not for sissies.

Sherry Gore, Pinecraft, Florida

Luscious Lemonade Pie

1 (5 ounce) can evaporated milk
1 package instant lemon pudding
1 (8 ounce) package cream
    cheese, softened

¾ cup lemonade concentrate
1 graham cracker crust

Combine milk and pudding; beat on low speed 2 minutes. Beat cream cheese until light and fluffy. Gradually beat in lemonade concentrate. Add to pudding mixture. Pour into crust. Cover and refrigerate.

Anna Mary Stoltzfoos, Lancaster, Pennsylvania

Cakes and Frostings

Carrot Cake

2 cups flour	¾ teaspoon salt
2 teaspoons baking soda	3 cups grated carrots
2 teaspoons cinnamon	3 eggs
2 cups sugar	1½ cups vegetable oil

Cream Cheese Icing

4 ounces cream cheese, softened	½ teaspoon vanilla
¼ cup butter, softened	1½ – 2 cups powdered sugar

Preheat oven to 350°. Mix cake ingredients together in a large bowl. Mix well and pour into a greased 13x9-inch pan. Bake 50 minutes. To make icing, combine cream cheese, butter, and vanilla. Gradually add powdered sugar and beat until smooth. Continue to beat until light and fluffy. Serves 16 – 20. (See color plate 30 for illustration.)

Esther Schlabach, Sarasota, Florida

Amish Oatmeal Cake

1½ cups boiling water	1½ cups flour
1 cup quick oats	1 teaspoon baking soda
1 cup brown sugar	½ teaspoon salt
1 cup white sugar	1 tablespoon cocoa
½ cup shortening	1 cup chocolate chips, divided
2 eggs	½ cup chopped nuts

Preheat oven to 350°. Pour boiling water over oats and let set 10 minutes. Meanwhile, beat sugars and shortening well. Beat in eggs, then add dry ingredients. Stir in oatmeal mixture, and add ½ cup chocolate chips. Spread in 13x9-inch greased pan. Sprinkle remaining chocolate chips and nuts on top of cake. Bake 30 minutes.

Mrs. Daniel (Katie) Borntrager

White Chocolate Fudge Cake

1 white cake mix	1 teaspoon vanilla
1½ cups water	3 (1 ounce) squares white baking
3 egg whites	chocolate, melted
⅓ cup vegetable oil	

Filling

¾ cup semisweet chocolate chips	2 tablespoons butter

Frosting

1 (16 ounce) can vanilla frosting	1 teaspoon vanilla
3 (1 ounce) squares white chocolate, melted	1 (8 ounce) container nondairy whipped topping, thawed

Preheat oven to 350°. In mixing bowl, combine dry cake mix, water, egg whites, oil, and vanilla. Beat on low 2 minutes; stir in white chocolate.

Pour into a well-greased 13x9-inch pan. Bake 25 to 30 minutes or until a toothpick inserted in the center comes out clean. Meanwhile, in microwave or heavy saucepan over low heat, melt chocolate chips and butter; stir until smooth. Spread over warm cake. In mixing bowl, beat frosting. Stir in white chocolate and vanilla. Fold in whipped topping, and frost cake. Store in refrigerator. Makes 16 servings.

Esther Martin, Martinsburg, Pennsylvania

Tasty Cakes

2 cups sugar
⅔ cup butter, melted
1 teaspoon vanilla
¼ teaspoon salt
2 teaspoons baking soda

¾ cup cocoa
2 cups water
2 teaspoons vinegar
3 cups flour

Preheat oven to 350°. Mix all ingredients. Pour into two 15x11-inch pans. Bake 15 minutes. Cool. Frost both layers with Anna's Frosting.

Anna Musser, Manheim, Pennsylvania

Anna's Frosting

8 – 10 cups powdered sugar
1½ cups shortening
2 tablespoons butter, softened

1 teaspoon salt
1 tablespoon vanilla
1 cup milk, scant

Fill mixing bowl with 8 cups or more powdered sugar. Add rest of ingredients and mix 5 minutes. Makes enough for three cakes. Use for tasty cakes, doughnuts, and whoopie pies, etc. Keeps well in refrigerator for several weeks.

Anna Musser, Manheim, Pennsylvania

Chocolate Mayonnaise Cake

1½ cups sugar
1 teaspoon vanilla
1 cup mayonnaise
2 cups flour

2 teaspoons baking soda
pinch of salt
4 tablespoons cocoa powder
1 cup hot water

Preheat oven to 350°. Combine ingredients in order given and beat well. Pour into cake pan. Bake 30 minutes.

Mrs. Homer (Fannie) Lambright, Pinecraft, Florida

November 27, 2005
Pinecraft, Florida

We are relaxing a little after all the excitement of our family's double wedding. It was a very unusual wedding, with around 1,300 guests coming from twenty-seven states, three provinces of Canada, and six other countries (Poland, Germany, Russia [not directly], Holland, Mexico [Russian Mennonite/ Kleine Gemeinde people where Sarah had taught English for ten summers], and Honduras). The wedding service was held at the Bahia Vista Mennonite Church, with quite a few sitting in the fellowship hall. The reception was held at Philippi Estate Park. The park had adequate room, and we all sat outside in the open. The weather was beautiful. We didn't even need sweaters.

Joe and Mary Wengerd of Mom's Restaurant, with Vernon and Mary Ellen Miller and assistants, cooked the main meal, and Mary Ellen Miller (Mrs. Wilmer) was in charge of preparing the desserts. (They didn't have the traditional wedding cake and ice cream.) Our son Matthias supplied the meat for the reception, butchering two of his water buffalo, and Greg Miller did an excellent job smoking and preparing it. With Mom's Restaurant's special barbecue sauce, it was delicious. There were thirty girls who served the meal, eight couples who served the drinks, and ten couples who served the bridal parties (five for each table).

Coming back to the church service, a group of around forty men sang a number of songs before the actual service began, with Larry Diener as director. At the outset of the service, Nathan gave a word of welcome to all the guests, followed by an additional welcome and a prayer of invocation by my brother, Levi Sommers. John D. Martin from Chambersburg, Pennsylvania, led the singing. John Drudge of Wroxeter, Ontario, brought the first message, and Merle Flory of Ellensburg, Washington, the second. Lester Gingerich, our bishop, performed the marriage vows. Then Ludlow Walker of Homestead, Florida, prayed a missionary prayer of blessing over both couples. The sermons and the vows were interpreted into Polish, as the ministers were speaking, by Ben Nowakowski from Bradenton, Florida. Demetrio Perez was the interpreter for the Spanish-speaking folks. The Russian folks were taken care of, as they could understand the Polish language. I am sorry, however, that we did not have an interpreter for our guests from Germany and several from Mexico who spoke little English....

Four couples served as greeters or receptionists as the people arrived, and four couples attended the guest books and handed out programs. There were twenty-five ushers and nine car parkers, and there were twelve gift receivers at the reception. It sure took a lot of planning and organizing to accommodate such a large group of people. (Nathan had been on the Haiti board for several years and was acquainted with handling large crowds that come to the auctions.) After the wedding we thought of different things that could have been done differently and thought of some folks we should have also invited, but as a whole, everything went smoothly, and people received a blessing. God's presence was felt.

Vera Overholt

Marriage begins when you sink into his arms,
and ends with your arms in the sink.

Overholt's Pineapple Wedding Cake

2 teaspoons baking soda
1 (20 ounce) can crushed
   pineapple

3 cups whole-wheat flour
2 eggs
1⅓ cups honey

Preheat oven to 350°. Dissolve soda in pineapple and mix all ingredients together. Bake 35 – 40 minutes. Frost with cream cheese frosting (page 191).

Vera Overholt, Pinecraft, Florida

Mother's Best Angel Food Cake

2 cups egg whites (from 16 eggs)
2 teaspoons cream of tartar
1 teaspoon salt
1 cup sugar

1½ cups powdered sugar
1 cup cake flour
1 teaspoon vanilla

Preheat oven to 350°. Make sure all utensils are grease-free. Beat egg whites, cream of tartar, and salt until white and foamy. Add sugar and beat until stiff. Sift powdered sugar and flour, and add. Fold in vanilla. Bake in a 10-inch tube pan 30 – 35 minutes. Makes 16 slices.

Mrs. Levi M. Schrock, Arthur, Illinois

Pumpkin Butter Cake

1 yellow cake mix
½ cup butter, melted

1 egg

Filling

1 (8 ounce) package cream cheese
4 cups powdered sugar
½ cup butter
3 eggs

1 teaspoon vanilla
1 small (15 ounce) can pumpkin
1 teaspoon cinnamon
½ teaspoon nutmeg

Preheat oven to 350°. Beat together cake mix, butter, and egg. Pat into a greased 13x9-inch pan. Beat filling ingredients and spread on top. Bake 45 minutes. Makes 16 – 20 servings.

Miriam Good, Elida, Ohio

Italian Cream Cake

This elegant cake is a favorite at Mennonite weddings.

½ cup butter	1 teaspoon vanilla
½ cup shortening	2 cups flour
2 cups sugar	1 cup sweetened coconut flakes
5 eggs, separated	1 cup nuts
1 cup buttermilk	

Cream Cheese Frosting

1 (8 ounce) package cream cheese	2¼ cups powdered sugar
½ cup butter	

Preheat oven to 350°. Cream butter, shortening, sugar, and egg yolks. Alternate dry ingredients with buttermilk and vanilla. Beat well. Beat egg whites and fold in last. Bake in three 9-inch round pans 30 – 40 minutes. Mix frosting ingredients and add to cooled cake.

Mrs. Harry (Sarah) Troyer, Burkesville, Kentucky

We asked eighty-six-year-old Anna (Bontrager) Yoder when she saw Pinecraft for the first time. "I was twenty-eight, and it was 1952. What I discovered was, in Florida, the weather was warm and I didn't suffer from chronic sore throat." The farthest Anna has been from home was Israel. World War II was in full combat, and boys went to service in the United States. Her brother Marvin didn't think it was fair to the soldiers that they had to leave the States — so he joined the Pax Service (a program for conscientious objectors and, later, the inspiration for the Peace Corps). He was sent to Israel. Anna thought she'd like to go visit Marvin. "Dad didn't want me to go. Since I was not married, Dad thought he should take care of me. I thought I could take care of myself. I told him, 'Dad, I prayed to the Lord, and I believe he wants me to go.' I went to Israel for twelve days. When I returned, I said to him, 'Dad, I did it.' He was standing there, and though his head was held down, I could see he was proud of me, but he would never say it."

Anna was an expert at decorating wedding cakes for more than twenty-five years. Her own wedding cake wouldn't be baked until she was sixty-two years old, when she changed her name to Mrs. Mahlon Yoder.

Sherry Gore, Pinecraft, Florida

Homemade "Twinkies"™

At the time of putting this cookbook together, the company that makes Twinkies™ was going out of business. No worries, however, because even though these homemade "Twinkies"™ may taste a tad different than the originals, they're still every bit as good.

1 yellow cake mix	1 cup cold water
1 small box instant vanilla pudding	4 eggs
	½ cup oil

Filling

¼ cup butter or margarine	1 teaspoon vanilla
4 ounces cream cheese	1 (8 ounce) container whipped topping
2½ cups powdered sugar	

Preheat oven to 350°. Mix cake ingredients and pour into 2 greased and floured cookie sheets. You can also line cookie sheets with waxed paper. Bake 17 minutes. Cool slightly and remove from pan in one piece. Cream butter and cream cheese. Beat in powdered sugar and vanilla, then add whipped topping. Put filling between layers and cut. Makes approximately 24.

Laura Yoder, Sarasota, Florida

October 29, 2008
Sunnyside Amish Mennonite Church, Sarasota, Florida

Following the hymn sing at church Sunday evening, the youth gathered at Tim and Julie Yoder's for nachos and banana splits. After playing the game Apples to Apples, they all pitched in and wrote a letter to P.J. Yoder, who is serving at Faith Mission Home in Virginia.

Sherry Gore, Pinecraft, Florida

Banana Split Snack Cake

⅓ cup margarine
1 cup sugar
1 egg
½ teaspoon vanilla
1 ripe banana, mashed
1¼ cups flour
1 teaspoon baking powder
¼ teaspoon salt
⅓ cup chopped walnuts
2 cups mini marshmallows
1 cup chocolate chips
⅓ cup maraschino cherries,
    quartered

Cream margarine and sugar. Beat in egg, vanilla, and banana. Combine flour, baking powder, and salt. Stir into creamed mixture. Add nuts and put into 13x9-inch pan. Bake 25 minutes then spread with marshmallows, chocolate chips, and cherries. Bake 10 minutes longer or until browned. Makes 18 servings.

Mrs. Harry (Sarah) Troyer, Burkesville, Kentucky

Buttermilk Pound Cake

1 cup shortening
½ cup butter, softened
2½ cups sugar
4 eggs
1 teaspoon lemon flavoring

1 teaspoon vanilla
3½ cups flour
½ teaspoon baking soda
½ teaspoon salt
1 cup buttermilk

Lemon Sauce

1 cup sugar
½ cup lemon juice

½ cup water

Preheat oven to 350°. Combine shortening, butter, and sugar until creamy. Add eggs, one at a time, beating well. Add flavorings. Combine flour, soda, and salt, and add to creamed mixture. Slowly add buttermilk. Pour into greased 10-inch tube pan. Bake on bottom rack 75 – 80 minutes. Cool 10 minutes, loosen cake with knife, and remove to wax paper. Bring sauce ingredients to a boil, reduce heat, and simmer for about 10 minutes. Poke holes into cake and pour about ¼ cup sauce over top. Let set 10 minutes and add remaining sauce. Cool. Makes 12 – 16 servings.

Irma Bender, Sarasota, Florida

August 1, 2007
Sunnyside Amish Mennonite Church, Sarasota, Florida

A grocery shower/reception was held in the fellowship hall Friday evening for returning newlyweds Tim and Julie Yoder. Julie's parents, the Jeff Brovants, were present for the festivities, having driven down from Michigan, bringing a load of locally grown cherries along. Tim announced, "Everybody is welcome to stop in, just not all at once!"

Sherry Gore, Pinecraft, Florida

Three-Layer Strawberries and Cream Cake

2 cups sugar
1 small package strawberry
    gelatin
1 cup butter, softened
4 eggs

2¾ cups cake flour
2½ teaspoons baking powder
1 cup milk
1 teaspoon vanilla
½ cup puréed strawberries

Filling

1½ cups heavy whipping cream
2 tablespoons sugar

½ teaspoon vanilla
1½ cups sliced fresh strawberries

Frosting

2 cups shortening
8 cups powdered sugar

½ cup milk

Preheat oven to 350°. Grease and flour three 9-inch round cake pans. In a large mixing bowl, beat sugar, gelatin, and butter until fluffy. Add eggs one at a time and beat well. Mix flour and baking powder, and beat alternately with milk into the sugar mixture. Fold in vanilla and strawberries. Divide equally into cake pans. Bake 25 minutes; cool 10 minutes in pans then remove from pans and cool completely. *Filling:* Beat whipping cream, sugar, and vanilla until stiff. Fill each layer with ⅓ of the mixture and ¾ cup strawberries. *Frosting:* Mix ingredients and beat on low speed until blended and very smooth. Spread frosting around the sides of the cake. Make a pretty piping of frosting along the edge of the top of the cake. Gently spread remaining whipped cream on cake top. Decorate top with strawberries. (See color plate 22 for illustration.)

Sherry Gore, Pinecraft, Florida

Hummingbird Cake

3 cups flour
1 teaspoon baking soda
1 teaspoon salt
2 cups sugar
1 teaspoon cinnamon
3 eggs, beaten

1 cup vegetable oil
1½ teaspoons vanilla
1 (8 ounce) can crushed
   pineapple, with juice
1 cup chopped pecans
2 cups chopped bananas

Icing

1 (8 ounce) package cream cheese
3 – 4 cups powdered sugar

½ cup butter
½ teaspoon vanilla

Preheat oven to 350°. Combine first five ingredients (through cinnamon) in large bowl. Add eggs and oil, stirring until moistened. Do not overmix. Stir in vanilla, pineapple, pecans, and bananas. Pour batter into 3 9-inch greased and floured cake pans. Bake 25 – 30 minutes or until done. Cool 10 minutes. Remove from pans. Cool completely. Mix cream cheese icing ingredients and spread over cake. Sprinkle top with ½ cup pecans.

Mrs. Sylvanus (Mary) Hershberger, Millersburg, Ohio

Apple Pudding Cake

3 cups flour
2 cups sugar
1 teaspoon soda
½ teaspoon salt
1½ teaspoons cinnamon
3 cups diced apples

1⅓ cups Wesson oil, buttery
2 eggs, beaten
½ cup raisins
1 teaspoon vanilla
½ cup nuts

Preheat oven to 350°. Sift together dry ingredients. Add oil and eggs. Add remainder of ingredients. Grease and flour 13x9-inch pan and fill with batter. Bake 1 hour. Top with whipped topping. This cake is best if mixed by hand.

Mary and Ellen Miller, Pinecraft, Florida

Chocolate Jelly Roll

5 egg yolks, beaten

1 cup powdered sugar

¼ cup cake flour, sifted

½ teaspoon salt

3 tablespoons cocoa

1 teaspoon vanilla

5 egg whites, stiffly beaten

Filling

1 cup milk

1 tablespoon cornstarch

¼ cup butter

½ cup shortening

1 cup powdered sugar

Mix all ingredients together, folding egg whites in last. Bake on a cookie sheet 10 – 15 minutes. Don't overbake. Place baked cake on a cloth sprinkled with powdered sugar. Roll up. When cool, unroll and spread on filling. Reroll. *Filling:* Boil milk and cornstarch together; cool. Cream rest of ingredients and add to milk mixture.

Ruth Stoltzfus

Shortcake for Fresh Strawberries

1 cup butter

4 cups flour

2 cups sugar

4 teaspoons baking powder

2 cups milk

Preheat oven to 350°. Crumble butter, flour, and sugar together until crumbs are fine and even textured. Add baking powder and milk, mixing until blended. Batter will be lumpy. Pour into a greased 15x10-inch jelly roll pan or, for a thicker shortcake, use a greased 13x9-inch pan. Bake 30 minutes or until a toothpick inserted in center comes out clean. Spoon sugared strawberries over thick slices of shortcake and stack; the higher the better. Top with a mound of sweet whipped cream.

Sherry Gore, Pinecraft, Florida

Pumpkin Cake Roll

3 eggs	½ teaspoon salt
1 cup sugar	2 teaspoons cinnamon
⅔ cup pumpkin	1 teaspoon ginger
1 teaspoon lemon juice	1 teaspoon nutmeg
1 teaspoon baking powder	¾ cup flour

Filling

1 (8 ounce) package cream cheese, softened	1 cup powdered sugar
¼ cup butter	½ teaspoon vanilla

Beat eggs 5 minutes on high speed with a mixer. Gradually add sugar, beating well. Stir in pumpkin and lemon juice. Add rest of ingredients and blend well. Line a greased 15x10-inch jelly-roll pan with greased wax paper. Pour batter into pan and bake at 375° for 15 minutes. Turn cake onto towel sprinkled with ¼ cup powdered sugar. Roll up cake and towel and let cool. Combine filling ingredients and beat until smooth. Unroll cake and spread with filling. Roll up again and place on plate. Chill with seam side down.

Darlene Hostetler, Coshocton, Ohio

Wroxeter, Ontario, Canada

On Monday we went to Myakka Park with Leslie Covers and Matthew Martins. We enjoyed the trail that took us through the interesting vegetation of palm trees and other tropical trees and plants. It was so beautiful that we hiked it a second time. The children were pretty excited when two alligators came swimming along the river as we stood on the bridge. A man was fishing from the bridge, and as he was reeling in his 12-inch fish, an alligator leaped through the water and swallowed the fish!

On Tuesday we visited with Vera Overholt for a while and then went to

Mixon Fruit Farm and saw the orange groves. We drove out to the Gulf of Mexico for a few hours and watched the waves come crashing in. I helped the grandchildren pick up shells. It was hard to leave our lovely, warm Florida home on Wednesday morning. We had really enjoyed the tropical setting and warm days, and we knew there was snow back home, but we pulled out at 4:00 a.m. and headed north.

John and Elizabeth Drudge

Coconut Cake

1 cup butter, softened	½ teaspoon salt
2 cups sugar	½ cup buttermilk
4 eggs	½ cup water
3 cups flour	1 teaspoon vanilla
3 scant teaspoons baking powder	2 cups sweetened coconut flakes

Preheat oven to 350°. Cream together butter and sugar. Add eggs one at a time, beating thoroughly as each egg is added. Add dry ingredients, sifted together, alternately with the buttermilk and water which have been mixed together. Add vanilla and beat well. Stir in coconut. Pour batter into greased 13x9-inch pan. Bake 25 – 30 minutes. Do not overbake. Cool.

Fannie Kay Yoder, Pinecraft, Florida

Yellow Cake from Scratch

1 cup butter	½ teaspoon salt
1 cup sugar	½ teaspoon baking soda
2 eggs, separated	½ teaspoon baking powder
1 teaspoon vanilla	1 cup buttermilk
2½ cups cake flour	1 cup sour cream

Preheat oven to 350°. Cream butter and sugar until fluffy. In a separate bowl beat egg yolks, adding to creamed mixture one at a time. Add vanilla and mix well. Sift together flour, salt, baking soda, and baking powder. Add alternately buttermilk and sour cream to cake mixture. Beat until smooth. Gently fold in stiffly beaten egg whites. Pour batter into two 9x9-inch cake pans or one 13x9-inch pan. Bake 50 minutes or until toothpick comes out clean. Serves 12 – 14 using 9x9-inch pans or 16 using 13x9-inch pan.

Sherry Gore, Pinecraft, Florida

Chocolate Wacky Cake

Everyone loves chocolate cake. This one's a favorite!

1¾ cups flour	2 eggs
2 cups sugar	1 cup black coffee, at room
¾ cup cocoa powder	temperature
2 teaspoons baking soda	1 cup buttermilk (or sour milk)
1 teaspoon baking powder	½ cup vegetable or canola oil
1 teaspoon salt	1 teaspoon vanilla

Frosting

½ cup butter, softened	3 cups powdered sugar
2 ounces unsweetened chocolate,	3 tablespoons milk
melted and cooled	2 teaspoons vanilla

Preheat oven to 350°. Combine flour, sugar, cocoa, baking soda, baking powder, and salt in a large mixing bowl or stand mixer. Add eggs, coffee, buttermilk, oil, and vanilla. Beat for several minutes. Batter will be thin. Pour batter into a greased and floured 13x9-inch pan. Bake 30 – 35 minutes. Combine frosting ingredients and mix until creamy. Frost cake.

Sherry Gore, Pinecraft, Florida

Desserts

Key Lime Dessert

Crust

2 cups graham cracker crumbs
1 cup sugar

½ cup butter, softened

Filling

1 pound cream cheese
2 cans (14 ounce) sweetened
    condensed milk

⅓ cup lime juice
⅔ cup lemon juice

Mix crust ingredients and press in bottom of 13x9-inch pan. Beat cream cheese, then add milk until nice and smooth, then slowly add juices until well mixed. Pour over crust immediately. The juice makes it harden quickly. Top with thickened fruit. Blueberry and raspberry are both delicious choices. You can adjust the amount of lime and lemon juice to suit your taste. Makes 20 small servings.

Esther Schlabach, Sarasota, Florida

Orange Tapioca Fluff

2½ cups water
½ cup tapioca
pinch of salt
⅓ cup sugar
2 tablespoons Jell-O (any flavor)

½ cup cold water
2 cups oranges, cut in bite-size
    pieces
whipped cream

Bring to boil 2½ cups water. Add tapioca. Boil 10 minutes in a covered pot. Take off heat and let set 30 minutes. Add salt, sugar, and Jell-O; stir until dissolved. Add cold water and chill in refrigerator. Mix in oranges and whipped cream. Makes 6 servings.

Mrs. Paul E. (Mary) Yoder

Vanilla Pudding

6 cups milk (reserve 1 cup)
1¼ cups sugar (reserve ¼ cup)
½ teaspoon salt
½ cup (approximately 4) egg yolks

¾ cup cornstarch
⅓ cup butter
2 teaspoons vanilla

Bring 5 cups milk, 1 cup sugar, and salt to a boil. Do not stir! Combine egg yolks, cornstarch, and the remaining milk and sugar. Add to hot milk. When thickened, add butter and vanilla. Makes enough to fill 2 8-inch pies or 1 10-inch deep dish pie.

Mrs. Levi M. Schrock, Arthur, Illinois

My Favorite Cheesecake

Crust

1¼ cups graham cracker crumbs
¼ cup sugar

⅓ cup margarine, melted

Filling

3 (8 ounce) packages cream cheese
1 cup sugar

3 eggs
1½ tablespoons lemon juice

Topping

4 tablespoons sugar
1½ cups sour cream

1 teaspoon vanilla

Preheat oven to 350°. Mix crust and press in a 9-inch cheesecake pan. Mix filling ingredients until smooth, pour over crust, and bake 35 – 45 minutes. Remove from oven. Mix topping ingredients and spread over top. Bake an additional 10 minutes, then turn off oven heat. Leave in warm oven 30 minutes. Remove from oven and run a knife around edge of cake. Loosen and remove ring. Refrigerate several hours before removing pan bottom. Makes 12 – 14 servings.

Sarah Joy Beiler, Pinecraft, Florida

Peanut Butter Delight

Crust

1 cup flour

½ cup chopped nuts

½ cup butter, melted

Filling

6 cups milk

6 egg yolks

1 cup flour or ½ cup cornstarch

1½ cups sugar

1 teaspoon salt

2 teaspoons vanilla

4 tablespoons butter

Crumbs

1 cup powdered sugar

½ cup peanut butter

Preheat oven to 350°. Mix crust ingredients thoroughly. Bake in 13x9-inch pan 20 minutes, stirring occasionally. Pat crust into bottom of pan once it is nicely dry. Set aside to cool. Scald 4 cups milk. Beat remaining milk lightly with egg yolks. Mix with flour (or cornstarch), sugar, and salt. Add 1 cup scalded milk to this mixture, stirring briskly. Pour into remaining milk in large saucepan. Cook 2 minutes. Remove from heat and add vanilla and butter. Cool, stirring occasionally. In small bowl, mix powdered sugar and peanut butter until crumbly. Spread half crumbs onto cooled crust. Pour cooled pudding on top of crumbs. Top with 8 ounces whipped topping. Sprinkle remaining crumbs over top. Cut into 3-inch squares.

Mrs. Conrad (Linda) Miller, Sarasota, Florida

Cooked Chocolate Pudding

½ cup sugar
2 tablespoons cocoa powder
¼ cup cornstarch
⅛ teaspoon salt

2¾ cups milk
2 tablespoons butter
1 teaspoon vanilla

In medium saucepan, stir together sugar, cocoa, cornstarch, and salt. Slowly add milk; heat on medium. Increase heat to a boil and stir constantly until pudding is thick enough to coat the back of your spoon. Pay attention, because this happens quickly. Remove from heat, and stir in butter and vanilla. This dessert is delicious served warm in a mug, or served cold, after cooling for several hours in the refrigerator. Can be used as chocolate cream pie filling as well. Makes 3 cups pudding.

Mrs. Sylvanus (Mary) Hershberger, Millersburg, Ohio

Soda Cracker Pudding

¼ cup butter
2 tablespoons peanut butter
½ cup brown sugar
18 saltine crackers, crushed
3 cups milk

2 eggs
2 tablespoons cornstarch
1 cup sugar
1 teaspoon vanilla
½ cup coconut

Melt butter and peanut butter. Add to brown sugar and cracker crumbs; mix well. Reserve ¼ cup crumbs for topping. Place in pan, pressing crumbs to side and bottom. In a saucepan, combine milk, eggs, cornstarch, and sugar, and boil over medium heat until thickened. Add vanilla and coconut. Pour slowly over crust and refrigerate. When cooled, sprinkle remaining crumbs on top.

Sherry Gore, Pinecraft, Florida

Lemon Heaven

4 boxes lemon Jell-O

4 apples, peeled and chopped

1 cup crushed pineapple, drained

Topping

½ cup sugar, rounded

2 tablespoons cornstarch

1 cup pineapple juice

1 egg, slightly beaten

1 cup nondairy whipped topping

Prepare Jell-O as usual. Once Jell-O has set, add apples and pineapple, and pour into 13x9-inch serving dish. Cook first 4 topping ingredients over low heat, stirring constantly until smooth and thick. Cool and fold in whipped topping. Spread over Jell-O. Makes 16 servings.

Mrs. Alvin (Irene) Miller, Pinecraft, Florida

Graham Cracker Banana Fluff

1 package unflavored gelatin

⅓ cup cold water

½ cup sugar

¾ cup rich milk

2 egg yolks

1 teaspoon vanilla

2 egg whites, beaten

1 cup cream, whipped

1½ tablespoons butter

3 tablespoons brown sugar

12 graham crackers, crushed

Dissolve gelatin in water. Mix sugar, milk, and egg yolks together. Bring to a boil and cook 1 minute in a double boiler, stirring constantly. Remove from heat, and add gelatin and vanilla. Chill until mixture thickens. Add egg whites and whipped cream. Melt butter, and mix with brown sugar and graham crackers. Line bottom of 13x9-inch pan or oblong 8-quart baking dish with half the crumbs. Spread pudding on top, then sprinkle with remaining crumbs. Set in a cool place to chill.

Mary Ellen Miller, Pleasantville, Tennessee

Molded Tropical Cream

1 cup sour cream
1 cup heavy whipping cream
¾ cup sugar
1 tablespoon unflavored gelatin

¼ cup water
1 (8 ounce) package cream cheese
½ teaspoon vanilla
2 – 3 quarts tropical fruit

Brush a 4-cup mold with oil. Combine sour cream and heavy whipping cream in a saucepan. Beat in sugar and place on very low heat until sugar is dissolved. Sprinkle gelatin over water to dissolve. Stir in warm cream mixture. Remove from heat and beat cream cheese until smooth. Stir slowly into cream mixture with vanilla. Beat thoroughly and pour into mold. Chill and serve on a platter with tropical fruit. The longer it sets, the smoother and richer it gets. Delicious.

Mrs. Fremon (Sarah) Miller, Walnut Creek, Ohio

Strawberry Pretzel Salad

Base

1½ cups crushed pretzels

½ cup margarine

Filling

1 (8 ounce) package cream cheese
1 cup sugar

2⅓ cups nondairy whipped
topping

Strawberry Layer

6 ounces strawberry Jell-O
2 cups boiling water

2 cups frozen strawberries

Mix pretzels and margarine, and press into an 8x8-inch baking pan. Bake at 375° 10 minutes. Cool. Beat together cream cheese, sugar, and nondairy whipped topping. Spread on pretzel crust. Dissolve Jell-O in boiling water; add strawberries. Stir until syrupy, then spread on top of cream cheese filling. Top with nondairy whipped topping if desired. Makes 9 – 10 servings.

Sovilla Mast, Pinecraft, Florida

Baked Apple Pudding

1 cup sugar	1 tablespoon butter
1¼ cups flour	1 teaspoon soda
¼ teaspoon salt	½ teaspoon cinnamon
2 tablespoons sour milk	1½ cups chopped apples

Preheat oven to 350°. Combine all ingredients and bake in 8x8-inch pan. Makes 9 – 10 servings.

Mrs. Mary A. Miller, Millersburg, Ohio

Sweetheart Pudding

Crust

2½ cups graham cracker crumbs	⅔ cup butter, melted
⅓ cup sugar	

Filling

1 cup sugar	4 cups milk
3 tablespoons flour	1 teaspoon vanilla
3 eggs, beaten	nondairy whipped topping
¼ cup milk, scant	

Mix crust ingredients well and press into oblong dish. Reserve some crumbs for topping. Mix sugar, flour, eggs, and ¼ cup milk well. Heat remaining milk and add sugar/flour mixture. Stir until thickened; add vanilla and cool. Spread on top of crust. Spread with whipped topping and sprinkle with the reserved crumbs.

Mrs. Daniel (Katie) Borntrager

Date Pudding

1 cup chopped dates	1 egg
1 cup boiling water	½ cup pecans
1 teaspoon soda	1 cup flour
1 tablespoon butter	whipped topping
1 cup sugar	bananas

Mix first four ingredients (through butter) together and let cool. Mix sugar, egg, pecans, and flour together, and add date mixture. Stir with a spoon. Bake in 8x8-inch greased pan. To serve, layer pudding with whipped topping and bananas.

Mrs. Lester (Sarah) Gingerich, Sarasota, Florida

Upside Down Cinnamon Pudding Cake

2¾ cups brown sugar, packed	2 teaspoons baking powder
3 tablespoons butter	2½ teaspoons cinnamon
2½ cups cold water	2 tablespoons butter
2 cups flour	1 cup brown sugar
½ teaspoon salt	1¼ cups milk

Preheat oven to 350°. Combine 2¾ cups brown sugar, 3 tablespoons butter, and water. Bring to a boil. Cool. Sift flour, salt, baking powder, and cinnamon together. Cream 2 tablespoons butter and 1 cup brown sugar together. Add to dry ingredients, mix well, and add milk. Spread into greased 13x9-inch pan. Pour cooled brown sugar mixture over the unbaked batter. Optional: Sprinkle ½ cup chopped nuts over the unbaked batter. Bake 35 – 40 minutes. Serve warm with ice cream or whipped cream.

Mrs. Conrad (Linda) Miller, Sarasota, Florida

Peach Delight

Crust

6 tablespoons butter, melted   1½ cups graham cracker crumbs

Filling

1 (8 ounce) package cream cheese   1 cup powdered sugar
1 cup whipped topping

Topping

2 cups water   4 tablespoons light corn syrup
4 tablespoons cornstarch   1 small box peach Jell-O
  (or Clear Jel)   1 quart peaches, cut up
2 cups sugar

Preheat oven to 350°. Mix crust ingredients and press into 13x9-inch pan. Bake 10 minutes. Allow crust to cool. Beat cream cheese until smooth. Add whipped topping and powdered sugar. Beat until well-blended, and spread over cooled crust. Combine water and cornstarch in a pan and bring to a boil. Boil for about 2 minutes or until mixture is basically clear. Remove from heat and add sugar, syrup, and Jell-O. Mix well. When slightly cooled and starting to thicken, add cut-up peaches. Spread over cream cheese mixture and let chill several hours or until firm. Makes 18 servings.

Mrs. Bill (Ruth) Yoder, Sarasota, Florida

Raspberry Cheesecake

Crust

15 graham crackers
¼ cup plus 2 tablespoons sugar

½ cup butter, melted

Filling

2 (8 ounce) packages cream
   cheese, softened
⅔ cup sugar
2 cups sour cream

4 teaspoons vanilla
16 ounces nondairy whipped
   topping

Raspberry Sauce (optional)

20 ounces frozen raspberries,
   thawed

3 teaspoons cornstarch
2 teaspoons sugar

Preheat oven to 350°. Crush crackers until very fine. Cut in sugar and butter. Press into 13x9-inch pan. Bake 8 – 10 minutes. Let cool. Beat cream cheese until smooth. Gradually beat in sugar. Add sour cream and vanilla. Fold in whipped topping and blend well. Spoon into crust. Chill at least 4 hours. Combine raspberries, cornstarch, and sugar in saucepan. Cook over low heat, stirring constantly until smooth and thick. Makes 1⅓ cups. Spoon over slices of cheesecake when serving. Makes 15 servings.

Mrs. Matthias (Sarah) Overholt, Sarasota, Florida

May 21, 2008
Sunnyside Amish Mennonite Church, Sarasota, Florida

During the end-of-the-year Sunnyside School program, teachers Jason Gingerich, Sarah Ellen Mohler, and Rosita Schrock did a splendid job in leading their students in song and recitation, to the delight of all present. Each scholar was presented with a character award likened to the child's personality traits.

Matthias Overholt was asked to join special friend Sarah Ellen in the front of the auditorium as a blanket throw inscribed with words of appreciation for Sarah Ellen was presented to both of them. Matthias then announced what very few already knew, his pending plans to marry Sarah Ellen. Next Matthias sang. It was the same song he proposed to Sarah Ellen with, when asking for her hand while atop the seventy-foot observation tower at Myakka River State Park last Saturday. Sarah Ellen plans to spend the summer at home in Washington planning their September wedding.

December 3, 2008
Sunnyside Amish Mennonite Church, Sarasota, Florida

Beautiful weather prevailed this week until yesterday, the day of Matthias and Sarah Overholt's outdoor wedding reception. This event was long planned to be held at Myakka River State Park. With gusty Kansas-like winds, high humidity, and rain that afternoon, some of us wondered before leaving home if they would move it indoors at the last minute. Thankfully the rain stopped before the program began, though most people drove through some bad weather to get there.

Tom Visser, also known as Brother Tom, dressed in his signature red suspenders, sang for the newlywed couple. Tom is the protagonist in the book written by Harvey Yoder, "Brother Tom: The People's Preacher." Living in occupied Holland during World War II, a thirteen-year-old Tom was imprisoned at the same concentration camp as Corrie ten Boom. By the grace of God, he managed to escape and ran away. Today Tom and his wife travel the world singing and testifying of Christ. My family met him numerous times in Dade City at Mel and Martha Stutzman's farm. We remember him to be a delightful character, dressed in handmade wooden clogs.

Sherry Gore, Pinecraft, Florida

Orange Tapioca

4 cups boiling water	¾ cup sugar
½ cup small pearl tapioca	2 or 3 oranges
1 package orange Jell-O	nondairy whipped topping

Add tapioca to boiling water. Cook until almost clear over medium heat. Remove from stove and add orange Jell-O and sugar. When cool, add oranges, cut into bite-size chunks. Top with whipped topping as desired. Makes 8 – 10 servings.

Fannie Beachy, Sarasota, Florida

Grape Pudding

2½ cups grape juice	½ cup sugar
3 tablespoons cornstarch	

Stir ½ cup grape juice with cornstarch and sugar, and set aside. Bring remaining grape juice to a boil and gradually stir in the cornstarch mixture. Stir constantly until thickened. Pour this over warm cornbread and eat with milk. Also makes a wonderful ice cream or cheesecake topping. In Pennsylvania it is called "grape mush."

Vera Overholt, Pinecraft, Florida

November 14, 2007
Sunnyside Amish Mennonite Church, Sarasota, Florida

Pinecraft is a beehive of activity, as yard sale season has officially begun. Palm Grove Mennonite Church hosted a sale to benefit the Gator Wilderness Camp for boys. Mrs. Gary (Maria) made soup and caramel dumplings with ice cream as a special treat for the youth.

Sherry Gore, Pinecraft, Florida

Caramel Dumplings

Syrup

2 tablespoons butter

1½ cups water

1½ cups brown sugar

Dumplings

1¼ cups flour

½ cup sugar

2 teaspoons baking powder

½ teaspoon salt

½ cup milk

2 tablespoons butter, softened

2 teaspoons vanilla

½ cup shredded apple

In a skillet, heat syrup ingredients to boiling. Reduce heat to simmer. Combine all dumpling ingredients. Drop by tablespoonful into simmering syrup. Cover tightly and simmer 20 minutes. Do not lift lid. Serve warm with cream or ice cream. Makes 6 – 8 servings. Note: Need a last minute dessert? This one is quick to make and can simmer while you serve the first course.

Sara Ann Hostetler, Sarasota, Florida

Frozen Mocha Marbled Loaf

Crust

2 cups finely crushed chocolate cream-filled cookies

3 tablespoons butter, melted

Filling

1 (8 ounce) package cream cheese, softened

1 (14 ounce) can sweetened condensed milk

1 teaspoon vanilla

2 cups whipping cream, whipped

2 tablespoons instant coffee granules

1 tablespoon hot water

½ cup chocolate syrup

Combine cookie crumbs and butter, and press firmly into the bottom and sides of 13x9-inch pan. Mix cream cheese, milk, and vanilla well. Fold in whipped cream. Put half of mixture into another bowl and set aside. Dissolve coffee in hot water and fold into remaining cream cheese mixture. Fold in chocolate syrup. Spoon half of chocolate mixture over crust. Top with half of cream cheese mixture. Repeat layers and cut through with a knife to swirl the chocolate. (Pan will be full.) Cover and freeze 6 hours or overnight. To serve, cut into slices. Serves 12 – 14 people.

Mrs. Lester (Sarah) Gingerich, Sarasota, Florida

Cherry Fluff

1 (8 ounce) container nondairy whipped topping

1 (14 ounce) can sweetened condensed milk

1 (20 ounce) can crushed pineapple, drained

1 cup chopped nuts

1 (21 ounce) can cherry pie filling

Combine all ingredients in a large bowl and mix well. Chill overnight. Makes 12 – 16 servings.

Mrs. Paul E. (Mary) Miller

Fruit Pizza

½ cup butter, softened
¾ cup sugar
1 egg
2 cups flour
½ teaspoon baking soda

¼ teaspoon salt
1 (8 ounce) package cream cheese
½ cup sugar
2 teaspoons vanilla
fruit

Preheat oven to 350°. Cream together butter and ¾ cup sugar until smooth. Mix in egg. Combine flour, baking soda, and salt. Stir into the creamed mixture until blended. Press dough onto pizza pan. Bake 8 – 10 minutes. Beat cream cheese, remaining sugar, and vanilla until light. Spread onto cooled crust and top with fruit.

Shannon Torkelson, Alberta, Canada

Fruit Slush

2 (6 ounce) cans frozen orange
   juice concentrate
1 (6 ounce) can frozen lemonade
   concentrate
12 ounces 7-Up (more if desired)

1 cup sugar
3¼ cups (20 ounces) crushed
   pineapple
3 large bananas
grapes or fruit cocktail

Mix orange juice and lemonade concentrates according to directions on cans. Mix all ingredients together and freeze, stirring occasionally so fruit doesn't float to the top. Makes approximately 1 gallon, or 16 1-cup servings.

Kathleen Schlabach, Sarasota, Florida

Florida Orange Rice

2 cups cooked rice

1½ oranges, cut up

2 tablespoons white sugar

1 cup whipped topping

Stir, chill, and serve.

Esther (Burkholder) Souder, Danville, Pennsylvania

December 5, 2006
Sunnyside Amish Mennonite Church, Sarasota, Florida

Sunday, December 3, was the long-awaited wedding of widower Frederick Gingerich (Michigan) to Sandra Obispo (here). It was a blessing to have all four of Frederick's grown children and their families present for the ceremony. Frederick's son Donald and Abigail Overholt were the attendants.

Several days of work were put in by many hands to help prepare the traditional Belizean meal. Mary Ellen (Wilmer) Miller, Maria (Gary) Yoder, Emileen (Stanley) Mullet, and Erma (Richard Sr.) LaRaviere served as cooks. Rather than having servers, Sandra and Frederick graciously served each visitor their dinner of Ricardo chicken and potato salad. The tables were decorated with tropical fruits, which some folks gladly cut into. Thankfully there were no reports of hives, which apparently affects some who mistakenly eat the skin off the mangoes. Sandra hand-grated sixteen coconuts to make the delicious "coconut crust," a dessert that resembles and tastes like a fruit turnover. The sweet potato pone was a hit as well. Frederick and Sandra also labored over a special tasty drink made out of pineapple juice. It was fermented and had quite an unusual taste to most of those who are used to typical Amish fare.

Sherry Gore, Pinecraft, Florida

Apple Crisp

6 cups chopped apples	1 cup brown sugar
¼ cup water	¾ cup whole-wheat flour
1½ teaspoons cinnamon	½ cup butter
½ teaspoon salt	½ – 1 cup pecans

Preheat oven to 350°. Place apples in a shallow 8x8-inch baking dish. Sprinkle with water, cinnamon, and salt. Mix sugar, flour, pecans, and butter until crumbly, and layer on apples. Bake uncovered about 40 minutes. Serve warm, plain, or with ice cream or whipped cream. (This is a fast recipe to make a quick dessert.)

Mrs. Marek (Sarah) Alimowski, Northport, Florida

Creamiest Rice Pudding

1½ cups water	1 egg, beaten
¾ cup uncooked white rice	⅔ cup raisins
2 cups milk, divided	1 tablespoon butter
⅓ cup sugar	(no substitutes)
¼ teaspoon salt	¾ teaspoon vanilla

In medium saucepan, boil 1½ cups water. Add rice and stir. Reduce heat, cover, and cook on low 20 minutes. In a separate pan, combine the cooked rice, 1½ cups milk, sugar, and salt. Cook over medium heat until thick and creamy. This may take 20 minutes. Stir in remaining milk, egg, and raisins. Cook a few minutes longer, stirring constantly. Remove from heat and stir in butter and vanilla. Serve warm. Delicious. Makes 4 servings.

Mrs. Sylvanus (Mary) Hershberger, Millersburg, Ohio

The proof of the pudding is in the eating.

May 14, 2008
Sunnyside Amish Mennonite Church, Sarasota, Florida

While most church folks prefer reading *The Budget*, the most affluent in Sarasota subscribe to the *Sarasota Magazine*. This ritzy publication featured local Amish and Mennonite cooking in its April issue. The five-page article, "A Bounty in Pinecraft," shed a favorable light on our community, whole-heartedly viewing the Plain People as the luckiest, as we get to enjoy "having Thanksgiving dinner every day" with the good, old-fashioned cooking we are accustomed to. A recipe was given for Mrs. Jake (Laura Jean) Helmuth's peach cobbler, using farm-fresh ingredients. Mrs. Paul (Linda) Yoder laughed when I told her, "Your goats are famous; their milk was featured in *Sarasota Magazine!*"

Sherry Gore, Pinecraft, Florida

Peach Cobbler

Filling

3 cups peach pie filling

Crust

1 cup flour

1½ teaspoons baking powder

½ cup sugar

½ teaspoon salt

¼ cup butter or margarine, melted

½ cup milk

sugar (optional)

nutmeg (optional)

Preheat oven to 350°. Pour fruit into a round 8-inch cake pan. Combine first four crust ingredients, then add melted butter and milk. Stir until smooth then pour over fruit. Sprinkle with sugar and nutmeg if you wish. Bake 30 minutes. Cherries may be used in place of peaches.

Treva Slabaugh (Laura Jean's mother), Pinecraft, Florida

November 4, 2008

Sherry,

The origin of the Florida Pudding is this: Someone was in Florida years ago and had that kind of pudding, thus, brought the recipe along home to Ohio. It was, and still is, referred to as Florida Pudding.

We had it as a dessert when we were married twenty-nine years ago, October 18. So it's been called that for quite a few years!

Thanks much,

Mrs. Wayne (Wilma) Miller, Millersburg, Ohio

Florida Pudding

1 cup flour   ½ cup margarine
½ cup chopped nuts

Pudding

8 ounces cream cheese   2 small boxes instant pudding
1 cup powdered sugar   (vanilla, butterscotch,
1 cup nondairy whipped topping or coconut)

Preheat oven to 350°. Combine crust ingredients and press in bottom of 12x8-inch baking pan. Bake 25 minutes or until lightly brown. Cool. Combine cream cheese and powdered sugar; fold in topping. Spread over cooled crust. Mix 2 boxes vanilla, butterscotch, or coconut instant pudding as directed on package; beat until thick. Spread on top.

Esta Raber and Anna Mae Yoder

January 28, 2009
Sunnyside Amish Mennonite Church, Sarasota, Florida

The 2009 Haiti Benefit Auction is history, and I missed it. I did hear there was fire in one of the Haiti tents at about 2:30 a.m. One of the dozen or so roasters was accidentally left plugged in and shorted, causing four potholders to catch fire.

    The highest price a quilt brought in was $1,600. Two quilts made during the sisters sewing at Sunnyside Church brought $750 and $950. John Troyer's quilt fetched $800. Some said prices were down this year, about 30 percent on the big-ticket items. Two hundred gallons of delicious homemade ice cream was cranked out of the hit-and-miss John Deere ice cream contraption, and 1,800 chicken halves were sold. The gross sale rang up to $165,000. The next Haiti Benefit Auction is scheduled for January 23, 2010.

Sherry Gore, Pinecraft, Florida

Homemade Ice Cream

5 eggs, beaten well
1½ cups white sugar
½ cup brown sugar
12 ounces nondairy whipped
   topping

1 box freezing mix (junket)
1 small box instant vanilla
   pudding
2 quarts milk
fresh peaches or other fruit

    Beat eggs and add remaining ingredients. Chunks of fresh peaches or other fruit makes this an extra special ice cream. This will fill a 1½-gallon freezer. Follow your ice cream machine directions. Freeze and enjoy!

Mrs. Sylvanus (Mary) Hershberger, Millersburg, Ohio

This and That

Dark-Chocolate-Covered Caramels with Sea Salt

1 cup sugar
1 cup unsalted butter
1 cup dark corn syrup
1 (14-oz.) can sweetened
    condensed milk
1 teaspoon vanilla

1 (12 ounce) package dark
    chocolate morsels
2 tablespoons shortening
parchment paper
sea salt

Bring first three ingredients to a boil in a saucepan over medium heat and cook without stirring, about 8 minutes. Stir in condensed milk, and bring to a boil over medium heat; cook, stirring constantly, until a candy thermometer registers 238° to 240°. This will take about 25 minutes. Remove from heat, and stir in vanilla. Pour mixture into a well buttered 8-inch square pan and let stand at room temperature at least 8 hours. Remove caramel onto a cutting board and cut into squares (about 1-inch cubes). Cook dark chocolate and shortening in a saucepan over medium heat 3 to 5 minutes until melted and smooth. Remove from heat. Toss caramels in chocolate mixture, in batches, until coated, using a fork. Dry on a rack or on parchment paper. Sprinkle with sea salt. Chill for at least 1 hour. Let candy soften 30 minutes before serving.

Makes approximately 4½ dozen candies. (See color plate 27 for illustration.)

Optional toppings: drizzled white chocolate, crushed peppermints, or sprinkles.

Sherry Gore, Pinecraft, Florida

Chocolate Orange Fudge

To make orange peel curls for a garnish, use a vegetable peeler to remove orange peel in a long, thin strip. Wrap peel around wooden skewer and let stand several minutes.

12 ounces chocolate chips	½ teaspoon orange extract
1 (14 ounce) can sweetened condensed milk	½ cup macadamia nuts, chopped orange zest curls for garnish
2 tablespoons grated orange zest	(optional)

Line an 8x8-inch pan with parchment paper. Melt chocolate and sweetened milk in double boiler. Stir until smooth. Add orange zest and orange extract. Remove from heat; stir in nuts. Pour chocolate mixture into prepared pan. Garnish with orange zest curls. Chill for at least 2 hours before cutting into squares.

Sherry Gore, Pinecraft, Florida

Freezer Fruit-and-Yogurt Pops

In a blender combine 1 cup chopped fresh fruit, 1 (5 ounce) container of vanilla yogurt (or plain), and 1 cup of your choice of juice or milk. Blend until smooth and creamy. Pour into 5 ounce plastic or paper cups, insert a plastic spoon (to hold spoon in place, push a piece of foil on the spoon and wrap the cup), then freeze until solid. Remove pop from cup by letting it warm for a minute or two and pull out by the spoon. (See color plate 23 for illustration.)

Some fun combos:

- Fresh mango/orange juice/yogurt
- Fresh kiwi/coconut milk/yogurt
- Fresh strawberries/milk/yogurt
- Fresh pineapple/pineapple juice/yogurt

If fresh tropical fruit is not readily available, use frozen from the grocery.

Sherry Gore, Pinecraft, Florida

Apple Butter

1 gallon apple cider or juice	1 tablespoon cloves
4 quarts apples	1 tablespoon allspice
2 tablespoons cinnamon	

Simmer apple cider down to approximately one-half. Slice apples and cook in cider until soft. Put through strainer (or peel apples first) and mash. Add spices to sauce and put in a large roaster. Bake at 350° for 3 – 6 hours, stirring occasionally. Can put in a slow-cooker on high for over 11 hours until right thickness. Makes 9½ pints.

Vera Overholt, Pinecraft, Florida

Caramel Corn

2 cups brown sugar
½ cup light corn syrup
1 cup butter
1 teaspoon baking soda
¼ teaspoon cream of tartar

½ teaspoon salt
1 teaspoon vanilla
6 quarts popped popcorn
1 cup peanuts, slightly roasted
(optional)

Mix sugar, syrup, and butter in a heavy saucepan. Boil 4 minutes without stirring. Remove from heat and add baking soda, cream of tartar, salt, and vanilla. Immediately pour over popped corn and mix lightly but thoroughly. Add peanuts if desired. Place on large cookie sheets and bake at 250° 1 hour, stirring every 15 minutes. Cool slightly and separate.

Mary Ellen Miller, Pleasantville, Tennessee

Brown Sugar Walnut Candy

3 cups brown sugar
1 cup whipping cream
2 tablespoons butter

1 teaspoon vanilla
2 cups finely chopped walnuts
2½ cups dried bread crumbs

Combine sugar, whipping cream, and butter; boil to a little more than soft ball stage. Let get cold. Add vanilla. When starting to stir sugar, add walnuts and bread crumbs. Put in buttered cake pan. Cut into small squares.

Fannie Beachy, Sarasota, Florida

Strawberry Jelly

1 quart mashed strawberries   2 cups sugar

Boil strawberries and sugar 15 minutes. Let cool. Can be frozen. (See color plate 9 for illustration.)

Susan Stoltzfus, Bird-in-Hand, Pennsylvania

Easy Yogurt

8 cups milk
1 tablespoon unflavored gelatin
¼ cup cold water

1 cup sugar
1 teaspoon vanilla
¼ cup plain yogurt

Bring milk to a boil. Dissolve gelatin in cold water. While milk is boiling, stir in gelatin and boil 45 seconds. Add sugar and vanilla. Remove from heat and cool to lukewarm. When lukewarm, stir in plain yogurt. Put in half-pint or pint jars, then on cookie sheet and into oven 4 – 5 hours at 110° until it starts to set. Put in refrigerator to finish setting. Serve with fruit or granola.

Mrs. Lester (Sarah) Gingerich, Sarasota, Florida

Orange Marmalade

3 cups oranges
1 can crushed pineapple

1 box apricot Jell-O

Chop oranges, peels and all. Remove seeds, if any. In a saucepan boil pineapple and oranges together 10 minutes. Measure and add same amount of sugar. Return to pan. Add Jell-O and stir. Bring to a boil; turn down heat and simmer on low until thick, at least two hours. Pour into clean, hot Mason jars. Wipe rims and seal with lids. (See color plate 5 for illustration.)

Susan Stoltzfus, Bird-in-Hand, Pennsylvania

Cheese Spread

1 pint milk

1¼ pounds white American cheese

Bring milk to a boil. Reduce to low heat and stir constantly while adding cheese. Stir until melted. Delicious on toast instead of butter. Also good on crackers.

Mrs. Andrew (Ruth) Overholt, Pinecraft, Florida

Zucchini Relish

12 cups grated zucchini

4 cups grated onions

2 red bell peppers, chopped

2 green bell peppers, chopped

⅓ cup salt

2½ cups apple cider vinegar

4 cups sugar

1½ teaspoons celery seed

½ teaspoon black pepper

1 teaspoon turmeric

½ teaspoon nutmeg

Mix zucchini, onions, peppers, and salt. Let set overnight. The next day rinse with water and drain. Heat apple cider vinegar; add sugar, celery seed, black pepper, turmeric, and nutmeg. Boil, then add to grated vegetables. Cook 40 minutes on low. Stir occasionally. Fill hot jars and seal.

Annie (Mast) Graber, former owner of
Dutch Oven Restaurant, Sarasota, Florida

Dear Sherry and Family,

Loving Greetings to you in Jesus' worthy name! First of all, a *big* thank-you for the Florida box! We had so much fun going through it — the children loved the candy — especially the saltwater taffy! Such a cute box it came in — Jerry thought maybe he could use it as a school lunch bucket! My pick was the coconut patties. Yummy!...

Love,

Joanna and Family

Hand-Dipped Chocolate-Covered Coconut Patties

Tastes like a fancy box of chocolates!

1½ cups powdered sugar

¼ cup butter, cubed

1 egg white

1½ cups sweetened, shredded
   coconut

1 teaspoon vanilla

1 teaspoon coconut extract

1 cup semisweet chocolate

1 teaspoon vegetable shortening

Add 1 inch water to medium saucepan and place it on medium heat to simmer. In double boiler (a bowl that fits tightly on top of your saucepan will suffice), combine the powdered sugar, butter, and egg white; whisk. Place the bowl over the saucepan of simmering water, and continue to heat and stir until the mixture is well-combined and very runny, about 5 – 10 minutes. Remove bowl from heat and stir in coconut, vanilla, and coconut extract. Wrap bowl with plastic wrap and refrigerate until it is firm enough to scoop, about two hours. Once coconut mixture has firmed up, line a baking sheet with aluminum foil. Place chocolate chips and shortening in microwave safe bowl and microwave until melted, stirring after every minute. Using a teaspoon, scoop small balls of coconut mixture and flatten them into patties. Using two forks or dipping tools, dip patties in chocolate and let excess chocolate run off. Place dipped patties on prepared baking sheet and repeat with remaining coconut candy and chocolate.

Sherry Gore, Pinecraft, Florida

Mike at the pretzel stand expects his trade to increase by 90 percent in the winter months. He used to be in the masonry business, but when things slowed, he took up pretzel making. The recipe is his own, made up from tidbits of information garnered from "the ladies here and there. They say it's the best pretzel they ever had."

Hasn't he heard of Auntie Anne's?

He has. But he stands by his claim. Besides pretzels, he plans to add hot dogs and cheesesteaks to help increase sales. I bought a pretzel and ate it. If the new items taste as good as the pretzel, then he is onto something.

Daniel Fisher, editor, *The Pinecraft Pauper*

Aunt Fannie's Soft Pretzels

1½ cups warm water
2 tablespoons yeast
5 cups flour (approximate), can use half wheat flour
4 tablespoons brown sugar
1 teaspoon salt

1½ cup hot water
2 tablespoons baking soda
melted butter
cinnamon sugar (optional)
coarse salt (optional)

Dissolve the yeast in water. Add the flour, brown sugar, and salt; knead like bread dough. Let rise 15 – 20 minutes. Roll and shape into pretzels. Dip into 1½ cups of hot water that has 2 tablespoons baking soda dissolved in it. Lay on absorbent paper towel to dry. Transfer to greased cookie sheets to bake. Bake 7 minutes in preheated 450° oven. After baking, dip into melted butter. We like to roll them in cinnamon-sugar or sprinkle them with salt. These are fun to make when you have several helping hands. Makes 10 pretzels.

Fannie (Earl) Miller, Sarasota, Florida

Fresh Fruit and Yogurt Parfaits

4 cups vanilla yogurt
3 cups fresh fruit

1½ cups granola

Using six tall glasses, layer ⅓ cup yogurt, then ¼ cup fruit. Top with 2 tablespoons granola. Repeat layers. Top with a few berries. Serve immediately. Makes 6 servings.

Sherry Gore, Pinecraft, Florida

Saltwater Taffy Pull

4 cups sugar
2 cups cream
1 tablespoon paraffin
2 cups light corn syrup

1 tablespoon gelatin, dissolved
in ¼ cup cold water
1 teaspoon flavoring, optional

Combine all ingredients in saucepan. Boil until candy thermometer reads 250°. Pour into 3 well-greased, large pie pans. When cool enough to handle, start pulling. Two people each take one end and pull. Continue pulling until an ivory sheen is obtained. Twist and cut with scissors into 1-inch pieces. Wrap each piece individually in waxed paper.

Sherry Gore, Pinecraft, Florida

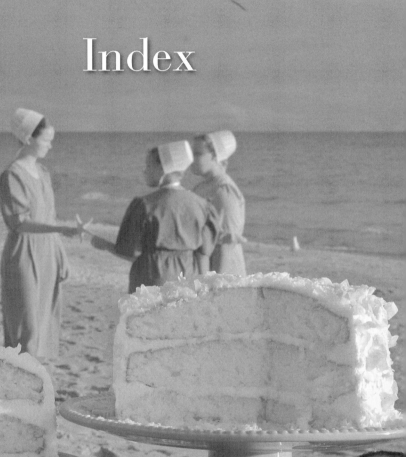

Index

Index of Recipes

Acknowledgments

Thank you to Vera Overholt, who wrote the section in the Introduction on "Who Are the Amish and Mennonites?" Thank you to the publisher of *The Budget* for allowing us to use material on their website in the "What Is *The Budget*" section.

About the Author

Sherry Gore is the editor-in-chief of *Cooking & Such* magazine, which has been called "completely heartwarming and visually stunning" by Amish novelist Cindy Woodsmall. Sherry is also a weekly scribe for the national edition of the 120-year-old Amish newspaper, *The Budget*. The National Geographic Channel featured Sherry prominently in the 2012 debut season of their documentary series, *Amish: Out of Order*. Sherry is a year-round resident of beautiful, sun-kissed Sarasota, Florida, the vacation paradise of the Plain People. She has three children and is a member of a Beachy Amish Mennonite Church. She's a caregiver to her twenty-two-year-old daughter, a Sunday school teacher, a cooking show host, and an official pie contest judge. As an author and longtime resident of Pinecraft, Sherry has worked with local Sarasota County government and various travel groups to generate interest for this unique and beautiful village.

Notes

Notes

Notes

Notes

Share Your Thoughts

With the Author: Your comments will be forwarded to the author when you send them to *zauthor@zondervan.com*.

With Zondervan: Submit your review of this book by writing to *zreview@zondervan.com*.

Free Online Resources at
www.zondervan.com

Zondervan AuthorTracker: Be notified whenever your favorite authors publish new books, go on tour, or post an update about what's happening in their lives at www.zondervan.com/authortracker.

Daily Bible Verses and Devotions: Enrich your life with daily Bible verses or devotions that help you start every morning focused on God. Visit www.zondervan.com/newsletters.

Free Email Publications: Sign up for newsletters on Christian living, academic resources, church ministry, fiction, children's resources, and more. Visit www.zondervan.com/newsletters.

Zondervan Bible Search: Find and compare Bible passages in a variety of translations at www.zondervanbiblesearch.com.

Other Benefits: Register to receive online benefits like coupons and special offers, or to participate in research.

ZONDERVAN®

ZONDERVAN.com/
AUTHORTRACKER
follow your favorite authors